RUNNING TALL

RUNNING TALL

Sally Gunnell
and
Christopher Priest

BLOOMSBURY

First published in 1994 by
Bloomsbury Publishing Ltd
2 Soho Square
London W1V 5DE

Copyright © by Sally Gunnell 1994

The moral right of the author has been asserted

A copy of the CIP entry for this book is available from the British Library

ISBN 0 7475 17177

10 9 8 7 6 5 4 3 2 1

Typeset by Hewer Text Composition Services, Edinburgh
Printed in Great Britain by Clays Ltd, St Ives plc

This book is dedicated to my husband Jonathan who has been my guide and inner strength over the past nine years. You are always there when needed, giving me so much love and encouragement.

I will always love you.

Contents

Prologue

My coach once said to me, 'Run tall, Sally.'

He showed me how. He meant that he wanted me to stay upright as I ran, keeping my back and hips straight, taking the hurdles by striding across them, not hopping over them. He meant I shouldn't lean into the run when I was going flat out, and he meant I must not let myself sag as I began to get tired.

Then he said, 'Relax, Sally.'

He meant I should stay upright as I ran, but to do it naturally, to make that the way I ran when I felt at my best, when I was happiest, when I felt I could win.

My coach has been saying this to me for more than a decade. He first said it when I was a schoolgirl running for my local club, and he said it the first time I entered an international event, and he said it just before I went into the stadium at my first Olympics.

He still says it, but not so many times that it becomes familiar and unheard, like a casual greeting or farewell. It always slightly surprises me, works its tonic effect. I know he thinks a reminder will help me through the next obstacle, or will urge me to some new target. I hear him say it when the

1

weather's cold or rainy, or when the future holds little more than another few months of seemingly ceaseless training, or when I'm fatigued or I'm losing my concentration.

Because I know what he means I find that my body hones itself into shape, my mind concentrates on what I am doing, and in some indefinable way I become straighter, taller, faster.

My world narrows to the 400 metres of hurdled track that lies between me and the finishing line, and when the starting pistol goes I follow that slender pathway.

For the next few seconds I am, in the only way that matters, running tall through my world.

Chapter 1

Seoul Olympics, 1988

Because the life of a full-time athlete is one of physical stress and mental concentration, I often think back to the first and last major championships when I felt relaxed and happy for the whole event.

These Games were the first for which I had qualified, and consequently I was one of the most junior members of the British Team that year. I was twenty-two years old. I went with only one goal in mind: I wanted to do well enough to run in an Olympic final. I was under no pressure of expectations, either my own or those of other people.

Bruce Longden, my coach since my school days, always encouraged me to take the long view of competing in a major championship. You must have experience of the Olympics, he said, before you can hope to win an Olympic medal. So I went to learn. I needed to learn how it feels to be present at a major competition, and I also needed to learn about myself and how I might respond to the physical and emotional demands I would experience.

The Seoul Olympics were in effect where the person I am today began her career.

*   *   *

Four years before Seoul I had failed in my attempt to be selected for the Los Angeles Olympics heptathlon event. At the time I had not been all that surprised, but I was none the less disappointed. Even then, Bruce's idea was that competing in such a major event, just taking part, was more important than anything else for a junior athlete.

But here I was at last, circling over Tokyo in a jumbo jet after the fourteen-hour flight from London, and preparing for three weeks of gentle acclimatization before moving on to South Korea.

After the airport arrival formalities, we were taken in buses to what the Olympic officials described unappealingly as a 'holding camp', but which in reality turned out to be an immense country club for wealthy Japanese businessmen on the outskirts of Tokyo. This was called the Nihon Centre, and it was to be my temporary home for the next three weeks.

Set in wooded, rolling countryside, with the most modern sporting facilities freely available to all the visiting athletes, the Nihon Centre was a kind of sporting luxury I had never experienced before. My background was the more utilitarian training grounds and stadiums of Britain, a world I knew and was comfortable in because it was home. It made me no more discontented with Britain than a brief visit to a luxury hotel makes you unhappy with your own house, but it is undeniably great fun to wallow in extravagance if you get the chance.

We made the most of our short stay. All the British competitors knew that if it weren't for the Olympics we would never be able to afford to stay there. As well as an athletics track and an Olympic-standard pool, it had a gymnasium, a golf course, tennis courts, jacuzzis – everything you could possibly want for the improvement of the body or the easing of the mind.

The accommodation, in a number of wooden chalets

dotted about the tree-lined hill, was perfect in every way
. . . apart from the lower forms of wildlife already in
occupation. I've never seen so many creepy-crawlies in
my life! The chalets were full of cockroaches, the big black
sort that live in tree-bark and go into buildings at night. I
was sharing with Kim Hagger, the heptathlete, and every
evening, when we left the others to go back to our room,
we would do the cockroach run, trying to find and get rid of
all the horrors that had crawled inside in the darkness. They
seemed massive and indestructible, with their armour-plated
backs and their vile scuttling movements.

If there had only been cockroaches it would have been
bad enough, but there were also snakes in the trees; one
day we found one of these slithering slowly across the steps
outside. On another night we were visited by a spider,
a massive black tarantula. This was the last straw. Our
screams brought several people running, who then valiantly
attempted to catch the unfortunate creature.

But the funny thing was that none of this spoiled the
enjoyment of being there, and in fact, because it was all
so exotic, it rather added to the fun. I'll never forget those
long peaceful evenings in the wooded hills, with the air
humid and still, and unseen crickets screeching in the tree
branches.

Kim and I hung around with a small group consisting
of Linford Christie, Colin Jackson, Sallyanne Short, John
Herbert and Joanne Mulliner. Of course we trained during
the days, but the evenings were our own, and we had a
great time together. Most evenings we ended up playing
Monopoly, or some other board game familiar to us from
childhood, until about two in the morning.

The stay at Nihon was further evidence that the British
Olympic team is one of the best organized of all. Once they
get behind you they look after you. Doubtless other countries

5

made similar arrangements of their own, presumably at other holding camps somewhere in the Far East, but I can't imagine that many other teams had such a congenial or businesslike preparatory stay in those two weeks. There was only one other team in Nihon with us, and that was the one from the USA. The Americans' care of their sportsmen is legendary, so the standard of the facilities was superb.

We trained every day. The team had its own national athletics coach, but in addition Bruce was out there too, acting as my own individual coach. With the daily training routines, and the simple but enjoyable social life in the evenings, we didn't feel under much compulsion to get out and see the sights of Tokyo. We did go into Disneyworld one day, but that was about it.

Some people might feel surprised at this, but we were at the camp to work, and foremost in all our minds was the prospect of the greatest athletic competition of all, and the precious chance we had been given to compete in it.

At 300 metres, the Nihon track wasn't quite up to Olympic standard (which is 400 metres), but it was fine for training. We were there every day, and although a lot of work got done there was also a certain amount of posing around. When the American superstars decided to put in an appearance (Florence Griffith-Joyner – Flo-Jo – was there, and Carl Lewis came in for a couple of days), no one else could get a look-in while they did their bit on the track.

The year 1988 had already been marked for me by a decision to change events. I had changed events before: I began my athletic life as a long-jumper, and as a Junior I had started competing in the heptathlon, but later I moved again, from that to the 100 metres hurdles.

One day in the winter of 1987/1988, Bruce asked me how I would feel about trying the 400 metres hurdles, another big move. I said I didn't mind, because what I really wanted to do was get to an Olympic final. I saw that as the next stage of my career, the next real test.

There was another factor too. The sprint hurdles is a 'glamour' event, attracting not only a huge number of competitors but also an immense rivalry and desire to win. Although I was by the time of the 1988 Olympics the holder of the British record for the 100m hurdles (12.82 seconds), on the international scene I was finding it hard to make headway. The probable reason for this is difficult to set down without appearing to be tainted with sour grapes, but in those days, just six years ago, the testing for drugs was nowhere near as rigorous as it is now. Some of the times being achieved by a few of the competitors, especially those from behind what was then the Iron Curtain, were noticeably fast.

I was ambitious and wanted to win, but the longer I went on the more it seemed that competing in the sprint hurdles was not the best of options for me.

For a time I trained for both events, and it took several months to get the hang of the 400m hurdles. We would alternate: one session would be devoted to the 100m, the next to the 400m. The way Bruce and I figured it at the time, because I was continuing to train for the 100m hurdles it wasn't too much of a gamble. But a funny thing happened: learning how to run the 400m made me better at the 100m! I had been trying for years to break the British record, but soon after I changed my training methods it was mine.

That wasn't all. At the end of May I went out and ran the 400m hurdles for the first time and I also broke the British record for that.

In fact, I was to break it five more times before going out to the Seoul Olympics. It had been for me a dream year, and by the time the Olympics came around we knew that switching events had been the right decision.

*   *   *

Our life of luxury at the Nihon Centre was all too short-lived, and in South Korea, just five hundred miles away, the Olympics were about to start.

Various groups of athletes began to fly out to Seoul, their departure dates depending on when their events were scheduled to take place. Those whose events were on the first couple of days flew out the week before. Mine came roughly in the middle of the fortnight, so I went across to Seoul towards the end of the first week.

Our arrival at the Olympic village (actually a number of brand-new high-rise apartment blocks, obviously intended for re-selling afterwards) was an unwelcome return to reality. After our sojourn in the luxuries of the Nihon Centre, it came as a bit of a shock to realize they were cramming eight athletes into every tiny flat. Kim and I again shared a room: there were two beds, and just one wardrobe for the two of us. Apart from a communal lounge, which had four chairs and a round table, that was it. There was a kitchen, but it was woefully inadequate for eight people and from the start we all realized that self-catering was not an option. All meals had to be taken in the huge canteen.

This canteen provided another gruesome shock for the pampered ex-residents of the Nihon Centre. There were always vast queues here, so even waiting to get your meal was a time-consuming process. And when we finally got to the head of the queue, the food was terrible. An attempt had been made to cater for the tastes of the cosmopolitan customers, but no matter whether you tried the Western-style meals or the Asian food it was pretty appalling. Jokes about eating sparrows, dogs and horses rapidly began to wear a bit thin.

After two or three gallant tries at this stuff, a few of us climbed into cabs and ventured into downtown Seoul in search of private-enterprise food. In the central shopping area we found familiar fast-food outlets such as McDonald's and Kentucky Fried Chicken. It didn't matter that we were exchanging one kind of junk food for another. It seemed to matter less because most athletes, including myself, routinely carry supplies of vitamins and protein substitutes.

Despite this, more often than not we ate in the canteen. It gave us a chance to meet other competitors, for one thing: if you're stuck in a queue next to someone for nearly an hour it's difficult not to fall into conversation! Also, the organizers had laid on for us several little shops, where we could buy personal essentials, souvenirs, postcards, and so on. There was also a computer room where you could dial in information about yourself and see how your bio-rhythms were shaping up. When I tried mine I found they looked good for my event. Make of this what you will.

When we were killing time in the Olympic village we would talk about almost anything in the world apart from sport. I was spending a lot of time with Linford Christie and Colin Jackson, and they were always telling funny stories, winding each other up playfully. When I was hanging around with the girls who were my flat-mates, it was much the same. To keep your mind on what you're there to do, you keep your conversation off it. We spend an awful lot of time at these big championships sitting around, and you have to keep yourself amused. Everyone would go mad if we held long heart-to-heart discussions about our events.

On the more serious side, because these were the first Olympics for twelve years in which both the USA and the Soviet Union were taking part, security was tight. All competitors had a pass, which they had to show whenever they entered or left the Olympic village, or at any of the sporting facilities where they were training or competing.

Bags were always searched. Guards were visible at the perimeter of all the principal sites.

The athletics stadium was actually in Seoul itself, about half an hour away from the Olympic village. We used specially provided buses to get from one place to the other, and once I had worked out which bus I needed, and the times it went to and fro, I had no problems with the system.

It soon sank in that now we had left the Nihon Centre the fun was over, and that there was not long to wait before my race. Just five days. I had done all my training, and if I wasn't ready now for the event I never would be. What I had to focus on was staying in practice, keeping supple, maintaining mental concentration.

The first thing I did, therefore, on my first full day in Seoul was to go to the track and check out where the reporting areas were, where the warm-up area was located, how I could get into the competitors' part of the stadium to watch other events, and things like that.

In the days before the first heat I would go to the warm-up area and try to pace myself towards the race. I would have a little jog and a stretch, do some strides (running at about 70 per cent stretch). Bruce was at the Olympics in his official capacity with the Norwegian team, but he was able to see me through one more track session, doing speed work. I was already trying to focus on the first heat, moving mentally towards it.

Four or five days is enough for this. When I went to visit the warm-up track for the first time I was instantly in the environment I know best: other athletes getting ready, going about their own business of staying in practice. We all tend to keep out of each other's way, but it's reassuring to be surrounded by so many people doing the same thing.

The 100m events are always the track events that go

on first. These are a great occasion, so I timed my own preparations so that I could get to the stadium and watch the heats. I usually make a point of watching Linford Christie's races, for example, and for a quite different reason it's a good idea to go and actually sit in the stadium. This is simply to get used to the size of the stadium, the feeling of being in there while an event is going on. On the other hand it's not a good idea to spend too long in there because in the summer sunshine it's hot and dry, and for an athlete dehydration is a constant problem.

After this I went back to the village. Already I was timing how long the bus journey took. A significant part of my preparation for an event is to make myself familiar with the practical details, so that when the time comes I can't be suddenly thrown off course by, say, missing a bus or not knowing where the toilet is.

None of this used up much of the day – three or four hours of it, perhaps. Having lunch at the canteen seemed to take almost as long! Many hours were spent lazing, chatting to the other people there, or catching up on some reading. There was a games room at the Olympic village, where we could play pool, table tennis, and so on.

But most of the time was spent simply being there in the Olympic environment, grabbing the chance to meet other sports people, not just from other countries but from other disciplines. Athletes rarely get a chance to meet swimmers, shooters, and others, except in these long informal hours while we are all waiting.

Two days before a major championship I take the whole day off, with no training at all, and I followed this rule in Seoul. On the day immediately before the heat I just went out and did a jog and a stretch. I was suddenly stricken with the most horrible feeling of despair. I felt completely lethargic, almost muscle-bound, incapable of movement. It was a feeling like nothing on earth. It was as if I would never be able to get out there. Why am I here? I asked myself again and again. I'm not enjoying this . . . I really don't want to do this. I started making excuses for myself. My leg's hurting! I'm too stiff! This terrible feeling made me depressed for most of the day.

Later, though, when talking to some of the others, I discovered that they were all going through much the same. It was just a build-up of nerves, and no amount of training can protect you from those.

That evening the computer produced the information about the heats: I found out who I was competing against, and in which lane I would be running. The ideal lane for the 400m hurdles is Lane 4 or 5. Lane 1, the inside track, is a little too tightly angled for hurdlers, while because of the staggered starting positions Lane 8 puts you physically in front of the other runners, which means you can't see them. Pacing yourself through the race becomes a lot harder in either case. Lane positions are normally decided by the seeding of the competitors, but in an Olympic heat the lanes are chosen by the computer, so it's all left to chance. I drew Lane 5 for the heat, which was lucky.

I managed to elicit this information fairly early in the evening, and therefore I had done most of the worrying before I went to bed.

At last the morning came, and because the heats were early in the day's events I had to be up early. I set the alarm for 5.00 a.m., but I had been practising even that for the last two days so it didn't come as too great a shock to the system. Before going to bed the night before I had laid out all my kit so I could get up and out with the minimum of disturbance to Kim, my roommate. Kim was very good, though. She heard me moving around, and sat up and chatted to me.

I was able to do the same for her a little later in the week, when her turn came around.

I went down into the cool morning, and caught the bus to the stadium.

Many people assume that every participant in every Olympic event is straining to take the gold medal. Perhaps this is largely true – I don't know: I can't read minds – but certainly it was not the case for me at Seoul. I had set myself what I thought of as an achievable aim: to get through the heats and run with the best.

For this reason, for me the qualifying heat and the semi-final were almost more important races than the final itself.

To qualify for the semifinal I had to come first or second in the heat, or, failing that (and therefore a bit more of a long shot), be one of the two best losers from all the heats. Once in the semifinal I had to come in the first four to get through to the final.

Riding down on the bus that first morning I kept my mind on the race ahead. The bus was full of other athletes, of course, several of them no doubt about to take part in the 400m hurdles qualifying heats, but I didn't stare around at my fellow passengers. We all keep our eyes to ourselves before a race.

When we reached the warm-up area I was met by the British national coach, who checked me off the bus and went with me into the area. Bruce was already there, and I went off with him for our last-minute preparations. To the casual onlooker, most of these probably seem to be completely undramatic.

Bruce had found me a part of the warm-up area where there was a bit of shade, and we went over there and sat down to wait. I spend a lot of time before a race just lying there on my back, doing nothing.

About two hours before the start of the race I began my warm-up. I always begin by jogging two laps, staying on the grass by the edge of the track wherever possible. After this I begin the exercises. These are designed to stretch, one by one, every muscle in my body. Next come the strides, maintaining a steady pace. By this time all my early-morning blues had been blown away, and I was beginning to feel ready for the race. I did some hurdles drills, going over two or three of them.

After a brief pause, during which I changed into my spikes, I went over to the warm-up track's starting blocks and practised a few starts. The immediate problem here was that all the other competitors were doing this at the same time. Again, to keep my concentration up I tried not to look at the others, just as, and for the same reason, they were not noticing me. Bruce was with me through all this, making sure the hurdles and blocks had been set up correctly and that no one was going to walk across me just as I was about to run. In these constricting circumstances I managed to get in a couple of runs as quickly as possible.

Then that was it. The warm-up was finished, and meanwhile there was nothing more to be done. I put my trainers back on, because it was a fairly long walk to the stadium.

From this point there was about an hour before the scheduled start of the race. The official procedures begin with the call-up, when you are supposed to check in to the reporting area. In fact there are two call-ups, separated by about ten minutes, and you have to report between the first and the second. Very few people rushed along when the first call-up was sounded, because no one wanted to be hanging around inside a tent with the thought that their competitors might still be outside warming up. Most people turned up at roughly the same time as I did: about three minutes before the second call.

Bruce walked to the reporting area with me. A man of straightforward and undemonstrative emotions, he said, 'OK, Sally, you know what you can do. Do it!'

I put on the number I had been allocated, then went into the reporting tent. The people I was going to be racing against were here, as well as four or five officials. These officials checked that I had on the right number, the right kit and the right-length spikes.

As soon as I could, I found a quiet part of the tent and lay down flat on my back, concentrating on the race, running through it in my mind, preparing myself.

When the time came, an official called us all to muster and then led us towards the stadium, carrying a placard. This had written on it: 'Women's 400m Hurdles Qualifying Round'. We trailed behind him, feeling a little self-conscious.

Although the stadium was right next door, there was a long walk ahead of us. The second reporting area was on the far side of the stadium, underneath the raised banks of the seats. We followed the official along a seemingly interminable corridor. I was looking down at the ground, just walking, trying not to think about the other competitors.

At the second reporting area they checked our numbers and spikes again, and then all we had to do was wait. I lost track of the time, but it must have been more than twenty minutes. The eight of us, highly uneasy in each other's company, sat or sprawled or lay on the ground, all thinking about the race. Every now and then we would get up and jog around, trying to stay warm.

When officials came to assemble us for the race they made us get into lane order: I was therefore fifth of the eight of us. Again we set off, crocodile-fashion, and again we had a long walk ahead of us, going around the outside of the stadium, under the overhang created by the banked seats. I kept my eyes to the ground, still intent only on not breaking my concentration.

We entered the stadium itself through the tunnel used by the tractors that haul the equipment in and out. Some people from the British crowd spotted me and yelled encouragingly. I tried to respond, but really by this time only one thing existed in my mind.

Once we were on the track there were still ten minutes to go before the start of the race. This is a really tough time. You are out in the public gaze, distracted by the wait and by the presence of the other competitors, yet sharply aware of the need to keep close concentration on the race ahead.

I could tell the others were as nervous as I was, because they were continuing to jog up and down as if to keep warm, though in reality this is a time when conserving energy should be a priority.

The starting blocks were already in position, as were the hurdles themselves. We had a few minutes left in which to check that the blocks were in the best position, and we each had one run over the first hurdle, but that was it. After this the officials made us go back to the start and strip off for the race.

This was the absolutely worst part. We had taken off our kit, there were still at least two minutes to go, and all we could do was stand there with several million people around the world watching us do nothing. If you have ever watched this bit yourself on TV you will know you can read the competitors' faces. You see what they are enduring at this moment: nervousness, stagefright, anxiety, frustration, impatience, pent-up energy. All these emotions are there in abundance.

Then at last the official who started the race warned us, told us, to get on our marks. Gladly, full of relief, we complied. We took up position on our starting blocks. Moments later the gun fired and we were away first time.

The actual running of a race is, I find, something I can hardly remember afterwards, and, now that I am faced with the task of describing not one but several of the races I have run, the reality of that failure of memory is a hard one.

There are reasons for this. Prime amongst them is the paradoxical fact that by concentrating so totally on the race in hand, by focusing on it to the exclusion of everything else, the details of it quickly slip from my mind. Only something totally unexpected (such as an injury) would break that concentration; I have been lucky so far in being spared major injuries during a race. Later I will explain more about the way I focus on a race, but for the moment it is enough to say that the closeness of focus on the job in hand makes everything else an unfocused blur.

Then again there is the inconvenient fact that in most important respects one race is like every race, and every race is like one. Only details differ: the names of the other competitors, the siting of the stadium, who won the race and who did not, whether or not I was pleased with my own performance, and so on.

Let me tell you how I would run a race, and think about it beforehand.

The 400m hurdles is run around one lap of a standard-size oval athletics track. The competitors run in lanes from the beginning of the race to the end, and because of the difference in length between the inner and outer lanes caused by the bends in them the competitors start from staggered positions. The athlete in Lane 1, the innermost lane, starts at the 'back', while the runner in Lane 8 starts 'in front' of the others; for the reasons I have already mentioned, neither of these lanes is a good one to be allocated.

There are ten hurdles to be jumped during the course of the race, and these are evenly spaced. Depending on the size and layout of the track (some are laid out in tighter ovals than others), most of the hurdles are positioned along the back straight. The sixth, seventh and eighth are usually positioned around the last bend. The ninth and tenth are placed on the home straight. It is only while taking the last two hurdles that each competitor can tell exactly how she is doing, because only these last two hurdles are placed in line with all the others. By this point, of course, the finishing line is dead ahead, so the race is being run at its fiercest.

For me the eighth hurdle is the significant one, because by the time I have crossed this I know exactly what the situation is. I know which of the other runners presents the greatest threat at this point; whether it is possible for me to win the race; or how much work I will have to do in order to maintain or improve my position.

From the off I run twenty-three paces to the first hurdle. I never count them during a race, but I have run those first few metres so often in training that there is no need to.

I don't run *to* the hurdle; instead, I let it come towards me. Some inner sense co-ordinates the length of the strides. As the hurdle approaches I can feel, I can sense, the remaining distance, and I marginally increase or decrease each stride to adjust to the correct length. I make no claim for special intuition or sixth sense with this: it comes purely with years of practice.

When I arrive at the first hurdle I take it with my left leg forward (my preferred position). I take fifteen strides to the next hurdle, and keep doing the same as far as the sixth. This means I can take all the first six hurdles with my left leg dominant. Between the sixth and the seventh, because I am tiring and starting to slow, I 'change down'. This means I reduce my stride rate marginally, to sixteen strides, and therefore then hurdle with the other leg. Between the seventh and the eighth I try to do another sixteen strides, and when I am on my best form, or I'm being pressed hard, I sustain that rate all the way to the finishing line.

At other times – for instance, when running in Grands Prix – I take fifteen strides to hurdle six, sixteen between seven and eight, then do seventeen strides home. In a big final I will keep the fifteen strides going as far as the eighth hurdle, before changing down to seventeen for the remaining two hurdles.

These numbers may sound confusing, but getting them right is what the 400 metres hurdles is all about.

In 1988, because I had only just started doing the 400m hurdles, and was rather unfamiliar with the race and the performance of the other women who took part in it, I was running each race as hard as possible. Five years later, when I was in the World Championships of 1993, I was saving energy when I was in the heats, and so I was a bit more relaxed. But in Seoul, at my first Olympics, I was running flat out.

I ran my heat more or less according to plan, and came third. The only thing that went wrong was that I 'stuttered' (got my stride pattern wrong) on the first and second hurdles, but this happened early enough in the race for me to make up ground.

In the semifinal the following afternoon, I got through to

the final by coming fourth, and while I was at it broke the British record, with a time of 54.48 seconds.

That night, and all through the following day (we had a day off before the final), I felt a sense of satisfaction and immense relief. I was not feeling complacent, but I *was* extremely pleased. Bruce was delighted with my performance, and so was I. I had shown that I had what it takes to reach an Olympic final, and in doing so had run well enough to please the considerable rump of British fans who had flown out to Seoul for the competition.

At the final itself, there was no pressure on me to do any more than the best I could; Bruce said to me as I went into the reporting area, 'Go out there and do as well as you can.' In his laid-back way he summed it all up.

I was placed in Lane 2, which I considered fair. As I came off the eighth hurdle and turned into the home straight, I was in sixth position. By giving it all I had got, I managed to pick up another place and finished very strongly. I was not very far behind Ellen Fiedler, from East Germany, who came fourth.

The winner was the Australian hurdler Debbie Flintoff-King. I saw this as an admirable win, one that made her a national hero at home, because at that time the event was so heavily dominated by athletes from East Germany and the Soviet Union. The silver medal was won by Tatyana Ledovskaya, from the Soviet Union. The bronze went to the East German athlete Sabine Busch.

I ran 54.03 seconds, my third British record in as many races. It was not fast enough to win a medal and it was a long way off the world record (52.94 seconds), but I was hugging myself with excitement at the thought of what I had done. My time was less than a second behind Debbie Flintoff-King's, and this was still a brand-new event for me;

the Olympic final was only the ninth time I had run this distance!

We all had to wait for the official results and times to come up on the board. I remember thinking, while I waited: God, I enjoyed that! That was great!

I was later to beat Debbie Flintoff-King in the 1990 Commonwealth Games, but soon after that she retired. We were never big rivals, but I was proud to have raced against her at this point in my career. My one acknowledged 400m hurdles rival now, and probably for the next two or three years, is the American athlete Sandra Farmer-Patrick. Sandra did not go to Seoul in 1988, and so our personal contest had not then begun.

But it was not for this reason that I enjoyed myself in the 400m hurdles that year. It was the absence of pressure, of expectation. I was just one of the members of the team, and I had a good result.

Nor was it my only appearance at the Seoul Games.

I still had the 100m hurdles and the 4 × 400m relay to come. Although I already felt I was moving away from the sprint hurdles, in favour of the 400m hurdles, I was nevertheless still the holder of the British record.

Fortunately, I had a day off between the 400m hurdles final and the heat of the 100m hurdles. I was still feeling good when I went to the warm-up track, where I met Bruce. I did a few strides, and a jog to try to loosen up, but I was still tired so I did not overdo it. I went back to the familiar idle routine of waiting: reading a little, chatting to some of the other people, trying not to burn out on the next race by thinking about it too soon.

The 100m hurdles heats were first thing the next morning, and although I got through to the semifinal without too much trouble I didn't do all that well in the second race. I came sixth, with a time of 13.10 seconds.

I think I was physically very tired, and mentally worn out as well. Going through the whole warm-up routine and the check-in is wearing, and it's difficult to pick yourself up again after a big race. I don't want to sound as if I'm making excuses, because in fact Bruce and I thought my semifinal was a reasonable run, and I had done much better than I had dared hope beforehand. After my 400m hurdles outing, everything was a bonus!

After the 100m hurdles semifinal, the next day I went straight into preparing for the 4 × 400m relay.

The team managers spared me from having to run in the heats, because I had already done a lot. The rules allow this. What happens is that you have to have two named girls who will run in the team in the finals, but you can have two substitutes in the heats. Another girl ran in my place in the heat, and I took over for the final. Sometimes there are arguments about the relay, because there are four reserves for the team. The girls aren't told which of them are going to be the four to run. Sometimes a girl will do a lot of work in the heats, only to be dropped in favour of someone else for the final. She might have been out at the Olympics for a week, there to take part only in the relay, and then after a brief appearance in a heat she is dropped. It is undeniably tough on anyone this happens to, but this is what athletics can be like. It's a competitive world.

I ran the third leg of the race in the final. I was not then very experienced, and the most capable athletes are usually put in the first and fourth legs, with the fastest 400m girl running last. Recently I have been running the fourth leg for the team, but in Seoul I ran third. We came sixth in the final, and felt pleased with what we had done.

For me, the whole trip to Seoul was one long learning experience. Judged by the medals table, I would not seem to have done very well, but there is so much more to the

Olympics than medals and records. Simply to have taken part was at that time the major event of my career, something I could tell my grandchildren, but as a bonus I had also run in two finals.

As we left Seoul for the long flight home, I knew that if I gave up racing at that point I could say I had done well. But I knew even then that Seoul was just a beginning.

Chapter 2

Childhood in Essex

My real beginning came as England won the football World Cup from West Germany, in 1966. I was born Sally Jane Janet Gunnell on 29 July that year. My parents farmed three hundred acres in Chigwell, Essex, and like my two brothers before me I was born at home.

If it is lucky to be born on a farm, then it is doubly so to be born on one on the very edge of London. We were less than ten miles from the West End, an Underground railway line ran close by the farm, and schools, businesses, shops and the other symbols of suburbia were clustered all around. But in the middle of it was our farm, a peaceful oasis of low hills and rich grassland. Very few of the commuters who swept past on the nearby main roads into London would have guessed we were there, and indeed many people in the immediate locality were surprised when they found out there was a fully functioning dairy and arable farm in their midst.

It was in this idyllic patch of countryside that I grew up. My father, Les Gunnell, had lived next door to a farm when he was a child and, for as long as he could remember, farming was all he had ever wanted to do. His first farm was in St Ives, in Huntingdonshire, but shortly after my brother Martin was born our family moved to the one in Chigwell. It was an epic move by all accounts: they brought not only all their furniture and personal effects, as well as a four-year-old child and a newborn baby, but all the animals from the farm, including a dairy herd. My father's father came too: Arthur Gunnell, my granddad, lived with us all through the years of my early childhood.

Before my eldest brother, Paul, was born, my mum, Rosemary Gunnell, had been a bank clerk with Barclays in Huntingdon. After she gave birth to me, and was also trying to cope with two growing boys, she had a daily help called Mrs Thompson. I have vague memories of seeing Mrs Thompson around the house, not really knowing who she was until I was a little older. My first actual memory is of a day at a local nursery school, which was in a lady's house and was restricted to about seven or eight toddlers. I remember sitting at one of those painting easels, in her front room. I must have been three or four at the time.

Childhood memories blend with each other. My brothers seem always to have been there, on the farm or around me in some way. Paul had been born in 1958, and for obvious reasons the eight years' difference in age between us was a substantial gap when I was little. I spent much more time with Martin, who was only four years older than I. In later life our relationships have to some extent reversed, as Paul is more interested in athletics than Martin, and has often travelled abroad to watch me competing.

Athletics runs in the family, to use a frequently repeated pun. Both my parents competed when they were younger, my father running and winning at county level. Unfortunately for them, however, the Second World War and its aftermath precluded the sort of opportunities I have been able to enjoy in the somewhat more stable recent past. By the time national and international competitions were getting back to normal, my parents were beyond the right age.

I have always benefited from their benign parental understanding of my sport. Once they realized how serious I was becoming about athletics they knew how to treat me. Because they had been through it all, they always gave me enough encouragement to keep me at it, but they never bullied me into doing more than I wanted. I've come across many instances of kids who were pressured into doing sport when they were small, but who felt the pressure and did not like it. Once they reached an age when they gained a measure of independence from their parents, they got out for good, which was not at all what their parents intended.

To get to the top you must always see athletics as just a sport, not a way of life, and you must not let it take over the rest of your life. For me, for many years, athletics was just a hobby from which I derived a great deal of pleasure.

Various articles and features in the press have depicted me as being obsessed with athletics almost from the time I could walk, but this is not strictly true. I was always physically active, and have loved sport – all kinds of sport – for as long as I can remember. Running, and other forms of athletics, was just one of many things I liked to do. In fact, it is very much an important part of my outlook that I believe it is a mistake to specialize in one kind of activity to the exclusion of everything else.

I spent most of my time outside school with Jane and Tracey Montgomery, girls of about my own age who were the daughters of one of the men who worked for my dad. There was another daughter I played with from time to time, Dionne, but like my brother Paul she was several years older and so mainly it was just the three of us who played together.

We led an outdoor life as much as possible, and because we

had the run of the farm we had a wide and varied landscape in which to play our make-believe games. On a typical day when we weren't at school we would get up at 8.00 a.m. to play all morning; we would come back for a quick lunch, go out again soon afterwards, return for tea at 5.00 p.m., and then we would be out until 8.00 p.m. or 9.00 p.m. We just played imaginative games around the farm. Many of these involved physical activity, but there wasn't an unusual emphasis on sports. We were healthy, active kids with a lot of space in which to play.

Just how non-sporting our games were can be judged by one of our favourite pastimes: setting traps and dares for each other. In several parts of the farm there were large piles of corn, or grass heaps where the silage had been, and we would dare each other to walk across them. In one well-remembered game we played there was a huge muck-heap where the cows had been. It had gone all crusty, and we dared each other to walk across the top of it. When it was my turn my Wellington boot came off, and got stuck in the appalling goo beneath the crust. I gladly left it behind, and leapt to safety.

Tracey and I played a lot of innocent spying games. Tracey's dad used to have stables up at their house, and they rented one of them out to this man who would come up and feed his horse. When he wasn't there we would move the straw bales around to make little concealed houses. Then when he came in we would be hiding, and we'd spy on him and make stupid noises at him.

At times I was left to play alone, and when I did I discovered the pleasures of solitude. I didn't have to walk far from the house to be completely alone yet safe from the predatory world outside. There was one particular hill I liked to climb. I would go up there, and it seemed to be miles from anywhere. I could scream my head off, but no one would ever hear me. It was good for letting a bit of aggression out!

Unlike many of the children I knew at school I didn't spend a lot of time in front of the television. When I did, I often found that the programmes inspired me into making up new games to play with Tracey and Jane. For instance, I loved watching *Superstars*, and instantly converted it into an endlessly variable set of challenges for our games.

I didn't do a lot of work around the farm, although Dad would have let me if I'd wanted to. I sometimes used to lend a hand with the cows at milking time, and when there were young calves I loved to go out into the fields and help with them. I would go out with Dad to bring them in when they were a couple of hours old. Because they were with their mother, the hardest thing was getting them to part company. I would then, by pushing their heads into the buckets, try to get them to drink the mixture of powdered milk we had prepared. I often used to help out in the morning with the cows, mixing up all the milk, getting their feed, giving names to them, and so on.

At other times I would go and join Dad, if he was using the combine in one of the fields, although most of the help I gave was confined to sitting with him in the tractor, or bouncing around on the trailer behind.

We children had six chickens to look after, and it was our job to keep the runs clean and to collect the eggs. We also shared a large, white and profoundly stubborn pony called Toby, who was with us for many years. He had been Paul's pony first, and then Martin's, before he finally became mine. I found it a bit of a bind having to get up in the morning to muck him out, and do it again after school, when it was dark and cold in his stable. He was the hardest pony to get going, and probably for this and all the other reasons I never really became very good at riding. Today this is something of a regret, because I love horses and would leap at the chance to learn to ride properly. Unfortunately, the risks of injuring myself are too great. Someday in the future, perhaps I will have the opportunity.

Once I started primary school my enjoyment of sport came into its own. I loved any kind of physical activity, and when I realized it could be channelled into competition with other kids, or into a team activity, or into setting targets for myself, then I began to live for games.

I was greatly encouraged in this by one of my teachers, Mrs Patricia Kaye.

Most of the kids lived in mortal fear of Mrs Kaye, for her reputation as a disciplinarian went before her. I too was nervous of her, but at first, because she was a form teacher for the older pupils, I did not have much to do with her. She taught us PE, though, and because I was good at this I began to flourish under her guidance.

It would be completely misleading to say she spotted me as a future Olympic contender, but like all good teachers she recognized my ability and nurtured my progress. Some years later it was she who suggested I should join an athletics club, and told me how to get in touch with Essex Ladies, in Woodford. Through all this, her fearsome methods continued. I remember, for instance, the way she enforced the school rule that the girls had to wear navy-blue knickers. She would send out all the boys, then make us do handstands!

The one thing Mrs Kaye taught me about sport that I have taken with me into adult life is the importance of enjoying it. Win or lose, I will always go on running so long as I enjoy myself doing so. If it becomes a grind, or when the need to win dominates everything else, then I will know that the time has come to get out.

The school itself – Chigwell County Primary – was situated

close to the farm. All I had to do was cross one of my dad's fields. It sounds an ideal set-up, but as I got older I found I wanted to walk home with everybody else.

This longer way round led past a sweet shop, itself part of the reason for wanting to go that way. One evening I was planning to go back to school after hours, because I and some of my friends liked hanging around the place when it was empty, but I slipped out first and bought one of those Calypso ice-lolly things, the sort that's sold in a triangular cardboard wrapper. I was still sucking at it by the time I was back in the playground. Just I was going up one of the climbing frames, the messy lollipop popped out and fell to the ground. As you read more of my story you will realize that this trivial incident is actually a symbolic moment: however seriously I take my athletics, I have never let it dominate my life to the point where ordinary concerns have had to be abandoned.

Throughout primary school I was doing as much sport as I could fit in. Much of this was completely typical of school sports: netball, rounders, and so on. I was also taking part in sports day, launching my athletic career with such memorable events as the beanbag race and the egg-and-spoon race. From the time I was about seven we also had little competitions with other schools in the neighbourhood, and I was always part of the team for those. My parents still have home movies taken of me when I was running then: my physique at this age was not the type you instinctively think promises a good runner. I was thin and gawky; my legs and arms seem to be all knees and elbows as I dash along. However, most of those old films show me winning!

Even today I do not have the 'typical' physique of an athlete. I am not as tall as many people seem to think, and although I have trained hard for many years, and used weights, I do not have huge muscles. For the record, I am only 5 ft. 5¹/2 in. tall (166¹/2 cm.), and usually weigh about 8 st. 11 lb (56 kg.).

I started taking part seriously in athletics when I was about eleven, and with Mrs Kaye's support I joined my local athletics club, Essex Ladies.

This was one of the first serious decisions I had to take in my life, because at that time there were two mutually exclusive sports that interested me and at which I was good: athletics and gymnastics. I could not do both, and following either would mean joining a different club. The decision was largely made for me by the fact that I had a friend at school called Jane Rolfe, and she already belonged to Essex Ladies. It seemed to make sense to go along with her.

Thus I turned my back on a possible future career as a gymnast, something for which I have never been sorry. I now know enough about myself and my abilities to be certain that I would not have made a top gymnast.

All this is a reminder to me of how many potentially first-rate athletes fall by the wayside, and almost always for reasons unconnected with physical ability. Of the girls I was at school with who showed an interest in athletics, or who were good at it, none is now still competing. Jane herself later went on to a different senior school from mine (we stayed friends for several more years through the athletics), but she is no longer competing. Eventually I got to know other girls of my own age at Essex Ladies, but none of them is running now.

One story is fairly typical: that of my friend Catherine Eversden, who was not only a member of Essex Ladies but who went to West Hatch, my own secondary school. I went around with her for years, and she was a great ally when, as properly training athletes, we ran at school. She and I were the only ones who went through the procedure of warming up before a race, something that would have made me extremely self-conscious had I had to do it on my own. I saw Catherine recently and we chatted about the old days. I asked her if she had any regrets in life. She said at once that she was sorry she had given up athletics. She had reached a certain stage, but at that point she wanted to get a Saturday job, and to do so meant missing the most important training session of the week. Something had to give, and it was the athletics that went.

I know for certain that all over the country there are hundreds of young men and women who have given up athletics in similar circumstances. They have thrown in the towel not for good or bad reasons but simply because the inconvenience of having to train so much of the time would mean sacrifices elsewhere in life. A boyfriend or a girlfriend could not be made to understand why his or her partner wouldn't be able to go out every Saturday night. A parent could no longer find the necessary time or spare cash to keep a talented child attending those weekly training sessions. Or a PE teacher changed jobs, and left a promising youngster in the lurch. These are all common instances. How many potentially medal-winning talents have we lost for mundane reasons like these?

On the other hand, there is no point regretting that which did not happen. In life there are many avenues you can go down, with junctions and side-turnings, and most of the time these decisions about personal direction are made with no thought of the future.

On the whole I think that is how it should be. Events have their own momentum. To give an example, it would be entirely wrong to point to an ex-athlete, now happily married, with a family, and say that the loss of that athlete to sport is a matter for regret.

Without trying to see everything about the past through

rose-tinted spectacles I would say that I had a happy childhood. I loved the farm, and once I had discovered sport at
school I was deeply contented there as well. I was never
much of an academic success, perhaps mainly because the
centre of my interest lay elsewhere, but I got by. If I
have a regret now it's that I didn't give more time and
attention to the academic side of school, but as I have
always said, I am a great believer in things turning out the
way they are meant to.

I suppose in objective terms I was quite spoilt as a child,
because I was allowed to get away with a lot. I was the
daughter Mum had always really wanted, after two boys.
I was also the youngest. In general I got on well with
my brothers, but there were times when war broke out
between us. I think it's unsurprising in a house where
there are three children. I do recall some awesome fights
– happily, they were always smoothed out in the end – but
mostly I remember the funny incidents: Paul keeping his
Easter eggs on a high shelf to stop Martin and me getting
at them, or the time the two of them decided my fingernails
were too long and held me down while they cut them, or
the many occasions when they would pull me under at the
swimming pool.

In spite of all this I did make one abysmally unsuccessful
attempt to run away from home. There had been an argument of some kind, and I ended it with my usual trick
of leaving the room dramatically, slamming the door and
stamping around in the rooms upstairs, just so everyone
would *know*. In my bedroom I found my vanity case and
filled it with all my cuddly toys. Clutching this to me I
went quietly downstairs and took a packet of biscuits from
the kitchen. No one was taking any notice of me. I went
outside, and walked quickly down the lane to one of my
favourite hideaways. I nibbled some of the biscuits. Time

passed, then more time, and still the expected search party did not materialize. After waiting a little longer I went back to the house, and everything seemed to be carrying on with remarkable normality. I waited for someone to say 'Where have you been?' but no one said anything. I must have been about seven.

At that age I hated going up to bed at night. The house was dark and spooky, especially in winter. Before climbing the stairs I would have to run across the hall from the lounge to switch on the hall light. This was one of my earliest record-breaking sprints.

We always took family holidays, the five of us, and we usually went to Hemsby, in Norfolk, where family friends, a sort of honorary uncle and aunt, had bought a seaside home. Most years we went there for our summer holidays, and sometimes I was allowed to take a schoolfriend with me: one year Susanne Cook came with me, and another year my athletics friend, Catherine, came along. At other times we cast our net wider: I remember one holiday in Jersey, and another in Ibiza, but neither of these has left much of an impression on me.

When I was eleven I started at West Hatch secondary school. Because this was further from where I lived, about ten minutes away by bus, I used to go with the other kids. I could catch the bus from the bottom of our lane.

I was able to do even more sports at secondary school. Before classes began; at every lunchtime; after classes ended; and in all the regular games periods: I was there in every possible team. As before, at the primary school, I got on very well with the PE teachers for the simple reason that I was good at the subject they taught.

I began to learn what might be called the social aspects of being good at something. In every school, in every class, there are the tough kids, the ones with an attitude, and my school was no different. To these kids sport was something almost beneath derision. Anyone who participated risked being sneered at; anyone who actually enjoyed it, who stayed behind after school for more, was contemptible in their eyes. It wouldn't have been wise to let on that I *loved* sport! This made it hard on me for a while, but in the end matters settled down.

One thing that helped was that, although I enjoyed most sports, it was only athletics at which I was really good. In most of the other games I was merely average or good. Some people were really good at tennis, or swimming, but these were two sports in which I wasn't very strong. I hated hockey, though I managed to keep up appearances. Netball and rounders were different, because many of the other girls were good at them, and so I didn't feel I was standing out.

Athletics, though, was my thing. All the time I was at school I was slightly embarrassed by how good I was. I didn't want to look like a show-off, and I was frequently tempted to hold back so that I didn't win by too great a margin. My best events at school were long jump, running and hurdles, and in all of these I usually only did enough to be sure of winning.

I don't mean to sound arrogant about this, because at the time I was in fact lumbered with the opposite problem – basic shyness!

The trouble was partly caused by my having started at Essex Ladies, because this was a real club and its members were treated like real athletes. I received proper coaching there, and one of the first things I learnt was that you have to warm up before competing, and you warm down in a controlled way afterwards. I always raced in spikes, not just running shoes. Generally the other kids would put on their kit, go out and start from cold. I would have been out there for half an hour already, preparing properly.

Because of Essex Ladies, the influence of my PE teachers at school was much less strong than when I was younger. My two coaches at the club, a Mr Sears when I was a minor, and, later, George Billet, obviously knew more than the PE teachers, who weren't athletics specialists. Often PE at school is a subject for which teachers stand in for each other, but not necessarily to the detriment of the games. At one stage, for instance, we were taught PE by Mrs Watson, a Domestic Science teacher! Even so, Mrs Watson took us for netball and we went on to win the county school netball championship.

As I grew older, school seemed increasingly to exist in the background of my life, because soon after I had joined the club I began to compete. First it was at club level, then at school county level, and eventually at national level. I was fortunate with my school. Once those in authority realized I had the potential to go a long way in athletics, they were understanding if I had, for example, to take a Friday off to go to a match over the weekend.

As the end of my school days approached, I began to appreciate all this and I decided to stay on as long as possible. This was partly to get a couple more O Levels (I ended up with four), and partly also to learn some secretarial skills so I would be equipped to make a living in the world outside.

But mainly I stayed on at school because it postponed the difficult decision about what job to do that would allow me to continue training. I was eighteen when I left school, and already by this age I knew that the combination of going to meets (many of them a long way from home) and maintaining a serious level of training meant that finding a job which would allow all this to continue was, to say the least, going to be difficult.

Chapter 3

Essex Ladies

In the mid-1970s, when I joined Essex Ladies, the club was based at Ashton Playing Fields in Woodford Bridge. This was two or three miles along the road from the farm, and Mum and Dad took me there the first day I went.

The clubhouse, a big hall by the playing fields, was shared with various other groups. There was a men's athletics club there too, but both clubs were independent of each other. At the time, Essex Ladies was in the top division of both the National League and the Southern League. They tended to waver between 1st and 2nd Divisions on the national scene, but were always near the top of the Southern.

I was still only eleven, too young even to be a Junior athlete, and so I joined the club as a Minor. This meant that for the time being I wasn't able to take part in the national championships, but I did go to a few open meetings.

As soon as I was twelve I became a Junior, and was on the lowest formal rung of an athletics career. At club level there are three groups where competition takes place: Junior, Intermediate (from age fifteen) and Senior (age eighteen and above).

The best advice any aspiring young athlete can be given

is to find out where the local club is, and to go along and join it. There will be no pressure of any kind, but all the encouragement and advice that's needed will be there for the taking.

Once I was a member of Essex Ladies I really began the slow process of learning about athletics, in a way that hadn't been available at school, even with a sympathetic teacher like Mrs Kaye. For one thing I began to receive the basics of proper coaching, so that I knew how to get the best from myself: how to warm up and cool down, how to look after my kit, how much time I should dedicate to training in any week, and other matters.

Best of all, I met many different people who had the same interests as I had. Some of them were youngsters like me; others were top athletes of their day. We all loved the sport!

And we would get out and meet other athletes, and compete with them. Once I had become a Junior, taking part in competitions became a regular feature of my life. On several weekends of the year we would go off to distant parts of the country in a rented coach. One of our frequent destinations was Meadowbank in Edinburgh: a long weekend with everyone, Juniors, Intermediates and Seniors, crammed cheerfully into the bus for the lengthy journey. We would stay at other athletes' houses, or sometimes we were put up in hostels. After the meet the return journey was another seemingly interminable one. When we at last got back I often found myself, late at night, queuing up outside the telephone call-box at Ashton Playing Fields, waiting to tell Mum and Dad I was home and could they please come and pick me up.

The coach took us all over the country. We competed against Stretford, Edinburgh, Wolverhampton, Hounslow, Bilston . . . too many to remember now. On every occasion we followed the same pattern: we left on the Friday afternoon or evening, competed on the Saturday, and came back on Saturday night or Sunday, worn-out but happy.

I'm still a member of Essex Ladies, and continue to compete for them whenever I can. I'm proud that last year we came about third in the 1st Division, although my contribution to that achievement was only minimal. As I'm rarely able to compete for them more than twice a year, I don't get involved in the leagues.

The competitions where I can be of most help are in the GRE League. Essex Ladies can get through the qualifying rounds without me, and I usually just run the final for them. This is at the end of the season, after I've done the Grand Prix meets and the national championships.

Nearly all the competitors in the British internationals do this kind of work for their clubs, and most clubs can boast at least one or two international athletes. The people I feel slightly sorry for are the young athletes who have taken the club through all the rounds but who, when the final comes round, don't get a run. The point here is that it's a club not an individual effort, and because the club wants to win they put up their best team for the big occasions.

Overall, there's a gain for the club. We won last year, for instance, and this works to the advantage of everyone in the club. It means that this year we will be going to Europe, and so everyone will have a chance to compete on that level. The first competition we're entering in 1994 is the European Club Championships, so in June I'll go off and do that one as part of the Essex Ladies team.

At the time I was involved exclusively with Essex Ladies there were quite a few top internationals there. Among them, for instance, was Sue Longden, who was then married to Bruce. Gladys Taylor was still running at the time. She built her reputation by running the 400m flat race, but towards the end of her career changed to the 400m hurdles. There was Joanne Taylor, who was part of the heptathlon group I belonged to. And there were Juniors such as Lisa Goreeph, with whom I was friendly for several years. Like me, she was a part of Bruce's training group.

The whole business of top internationals running for clubs can be a little problematical. It does of course work to the advantage of the club, but clearly there aren't always enough top-rank athletes to go round. In an ideal world each club would be producing its own internationals, but failing this some clubs have now taken to buying athletes in, if they can get a sponsor. Essex Ladies have never had to do this; other clubs have, but they will never admit to having done so.

Some clubs are better than others. You want to stay with the club that you've grown up with, for all sorts of excellent reasons, but it can be difficult at times. I've been lucky with Essex Ladies, because they realize that I should not over-race. The season these days is packed with events and many of them are ones I can't, or don't want to, miss. For the last decade or so, the IAAF/Mobil Grand Prix championships have been important to all athletes, and because these take place all over the world they can use up a lot of time.

Most athletes have an excellent relationship with their clubs. Linford Christie, for example, belongs to Thames Valley Harriers, which has always been good to him. On the other hand, Colin Jackson at one time was getting a lot of pressure from his club to compete, and he felt he really wasn't able to fulfil all the commitments. In the end he moved to a tiny non-League club. Everyone's pleased with the new arrangement. They're obviously delighted to have him, and he's happy to run for them, whenever he can.

Being involved with a club brings two-way benefits, although they can't be easily quantified. We wear club colours when we run in the National Championship, so at this point I become the embodiment of Essex Ladies. If I win, I do so for them, and only incidentally for myself. Also, if we win, no money comes directly into the club, because the sport is purely amateur. The appearance of an international runner will sometimes help boost receipts at the gate, though, so there's a bit of an advantage to the host club. For this reason, I suppose we concentrate on the home meets, to try to help out a little. The trouble is that at the height of the season these national competitions almost invariably clash with something going on abroad, so financially it doesn't pay me to do it.

Just as important is the fact that to prepare for a championship that really counts – the Olympics, say, or the World – I need a tough level of competition.

There are times when I do need my club. For instance, I might be in a period of recovery following an injury and want an easier race to help get me back on form. Or I might want to try a different event, maybe a 200m sprint instead of the 400m hurdles. The logical way to try this out would be by competing for the club.

Whatever the circumstances, my body will allow me to do only so many races in a year, and I have to be careful. However, I gladly stump up for my annual sub, and so it should be. The only thing that is a bit unfortunate these days is that because I live in Sussex, and the club is in Walthamstow, I can't get there for club nights. Those used to be really important to me, socially. We would go and hang out around each other's houses, and from the time I was sixteen there was a regular group of about five of us who were always together. That's impractical now, and I wish it were not so.

The club system in this country lies at the heart of the amateur status of athletics. Clubs are simply a concentration of like-minded people who love the sport in which they compete. It's all for love, and it's important that it should stay that way.

However, commercialism inevitably encroaches. Clubs need funds in order to survive, and to acquire funds they need sponsors. Essex Ladies, to take an example close to home, has recently been sponsored by Eastern Electricity, and this has helped a great deal.

The bottom line is that more sponsorship throughout the sport would keep a lot more clubs going. To keep going is the thing that matters most, and without sponsorship quite a few of the smaller clubs have gone to the wall recently. However, the introduction of sponsorship has resulted in many of the clubs no longer being strictly amateur. No one's making money out of it, though, and it is helping to keep the clubs alive.

Chapter 4

Training Begins

Bruce Longden says he first spotted me because I was doing well at one of the club meetings. He had come along to Essex Ladies partly because his wife Sue was a member, and partly because of his work. He was a national coach for the Federation, and it was part of his job to keep a weather eye open for promising young athletes.

I remember Bruce leaning over the fence and speaking to my father that day. He looked like a Very Important Person. I didn't know his name but I realized he was a national coach. Later, he spoke to me. He explained that Joanne Taylor, one of the girls I knew at Essex Ladies, was already training with him as part of the group he was in charge of at Crystal Palace. He suggested that I might like to go over one evening and join in, and see how I got on. He said he thought it would be a good idea if I went on one of the evenings Joanne was there. Dad, who had already agreed to this, volunteered to drive me there after school.

At this time I was training with the club coach, George Billet. Bruce made it clear that if things didn't work out, there was no reason why I should interrupt the training with Mr Billet. No one was forcing me to do anything I didn't want.

Bruce's most successful and famous athlete during this period was Daley Thompson, who was working towards what would become his Olympic gold in Moscow. To be invited to train with such an impressive coach was a tremendous opportunity, and nothing would have made me turn him down.

The result of all this was that I was soon a regular member of Bruce's Crystal Palace group, and once a week I would go down there for an evening's training session with several other young athletes.

I have not always been a hurdler. My first sport was the long jump, and this is what I was doing when I first joined Essex Ladies and when Bruce spotted me. He moved me towards the pentathlon, but for this I needed to know how to hurdle. Bruce taught me that, and I concentrated on the pentathlon for a while. In 1983 he moved me on again, this time to the heptathlon.

I am often asked for advice about the way a young athlete should proceed – how to find the best event, and so on. My usual answer is the broad one: that you should never specialize. Don't set out to be solely a sprinter, or a shot-putter, or a hurdler, or whatever. Take on athletics as a whole, and get as much enjoyment from the overall activity as possible. If you are particularly good in any one event, your prowess will become evident.

For this reason, my more specific advice is to try one of the multiple events: for young athletes, the pentathlon; for slightly older ones, the heptathlon. Both of these provide a testing range of events, where strengths and weaknesses will soon show themselves.

The five events in the pentathlon are:

Long jump;
High jump;
Shot;
800m flat;
100m hurdles.

The heptathlon has the same events, plus:
Javelin;
200m flat.

I believe that taking on these multiple events really pays off. You get a good overall grounding in track and field events, and in addition it teaches you the discipline of going out and training. With seven events involved, you do an awful lot of training!

Another advantage is this: because your ability in one kind of event will be different from that in the next, you learn how to win, and you learn how to lose. I have always felt I benefited from this, because no matter how good you are it's inevitable that you won't win every time you compete.

Some athletes find it hard to deal with failure; they take it out on themselves and those around them afterwards. In my case I soon discovered that I was really good at the hurdles and would collect a lot of points. However, I used to dread the high jump: it was almost always a disaster. Shot and javelin were as bad. But it was no good complaining at a poor result, or going off in a sulk, because an hour later I would have to pick myself up and run the 800m, or whichever one it was that came next. From this I learned: it's happened, so there's nothing I can do about it but go on and try to do better in the next event.

So, once or twice a week, from around my fourteenth birthday, I would go to Crystal Palace and join Bruce's training group. There were a couple of other girls from my area – Catherine being one of them – who were going there at the same time, so our parents were able to take turns in driving us. Sometimes it was my dad, or Lisa Goreeph's parents, or Joanne Taylor's. We would set off after school; I remember my dad would try to get through the Blackwall Tunnel before the rush hour began. We were usually all ready to start by about 6.30 p.m., and would train until about 8.00 p.m., while whichever parent had brought us either watched or went off to dawdle over a cup of tea; I know that my dad liked to go and smoke his pipe somewhere.

Bruce did all his group training for the sheer love of the sport. Although he was actually paid by the Amateur Athletics Association (now the BAF: British Athletics Federation), these spare-time training sessions were done on his own initiative. His real job was to go round and set up coaching courses in schools and other institutions, not work with individual athletes. This is still the work he does now. I was aware, even way back then, of how much I owed him.

At first, though, I was not especially close to him. I was just one of a fairly large group, and he paid me neither more nor less attention than he did anyone else. We would all meet up, and he would talk to the group in general, telling us what we were going to be doing that evening. Then, after we had warmed up, he would move from one of us to another as we did our exercises, never saying very much, just being supportive and encouraging. He always seemed to me to know everything about what I was doing, even when he was talking to other people.

I grew to know him better only very gradually. I think it began when I switched from the pentathlon to the heptathlon and Bruce was encouraging me with my hurdling. He would suggest that I watch other hurdlers and see their techniques. Sometimes I would make the trip to stay with him and his wife at their house in Crawley, then go with him for a full weekend of coaching at Crystal Palace, or in the neighbourhood. Our coach/athlete partnership began to form during this time.

On other occasions he and a small group of four or five young athletes would go off for weekends to Crewe and Alsager College, where there is a testing centre. These trips would not include everyone from the main group; there would just be the people he thought might benefit from this special training.

Slowly but surely, then, he and I got to know what each other was like. Nothing happens quickly or dramatically with Bruce; he always takes the long view, and builds up gradually.

Today, he is still working with groups of young people in much the same way, looking for the next batch of athletes, the ones who will inevitably replace me and my generation. Bruce is very unusual in this: there really aren't many coaches who find young budding athletes and, by providing steady encouragement throughout their development, are still working with them many years later.

This underlines a feature that is common to several of our current top athletes. Colin Jackson, Linford Christie and I – to give just three examples – have all been with our coaches for a long time. There must be something in this!

Success itself breeds problems, though, and, as the months and years went by, Bruce's training group grew steadily bigger. For several months he went through the painful business of trying to slim it down a little. At most of the training sessions there were twelve or fourteen of us, which is really too large a number.

By this time I was going to Crystal Palace every Monday night and Wednesday night, as well as sometimes at the weekends. I would also, on Tuesday and Thursday evenings, go to Essex Ladies and train there on my own. I was by then sufficiently familiar with Bruce's methods to be able, in effect, to coach myself.

Most of what Bruce has been coaching me has remained virtually the same for fourteen years. What has changed is the intensity of what I do, along with a couple of sessions that have been developed since I switched to the 400m hurdles from the sprint hurdles.

This changeover was the most significant of my career, because it needed a new approach to racing, how I plan and focus on each race, how I work out a strategy that will help me win. Earlier career changes, such as when I gave up the heptathlon in favour of hurdling, were minor in comparison. What I remember best about that was the relief of no longer having to do the shot and javelin, and, of course, the high jump.

The basis of my training now is two track sessions every week, which I have done all the way through my career; one is long and the other is short.

A lot of training is to do with recovery. For instance, in a typical track session I will do a 350m run, followed by a four-minute rest. Then comes another 350m run, with a six-minute rest. After that, I do 300m, with a three-minute rest . . . 250m, with a three-minute rest . . . 200m, with a two-minute rest . . . 150m, and finish.

I walk around during the rest periods, to stop the lactic building up. ('Lactic' is the name athletes give to an accumulation of fatty liquids in the bloodstream, which tend to congregate in the limbs. Lactic is caused by your body producing adrenaline when you're really working hard, then not being dispersed properly when you stop. The best way to work it off is by walking around for about five or ten minutes after a race. If you just sit down straight afterwards the lactic will probably make you physically sick.)

All the distances are timed with a stopwatch. Bruce does this, or if I'm by myself I can do it with a wrist-stopwatch. I prefer him to be there, though, because it's always best if someone else is timing you. And with Bruce at the side of the track, watching everything, I will usually do a better session. He knows when I'm doing my best; he also knows when I'm getting tired, and then he will encourage me to finish.

I don't train with starting blocks during winter. I use them only in the season and, even then, only if I'm running 400 metres and going over hurdles. In the winter months, I do no hurdling and almost no speed work. I use blocks if I'm doing speed work, or if practising starts.

In winter I warm up, then do my strides. By 'strides' I mean running in a straight line, at about 70–80 per cent of my maximum capacity. The strides that I do in winter, while preparing for the 400m hurdles, are probably faster than those I would do for a long track session of, say, 600 metres. On the other hand, if I was doing sprint work of 150 metres, my strides would be even slower. The strides just wake up your legs a little bit; they're not flat-out running.

Another kind of training is called fartlek. With this method, the athlete does alternating sessions of fast and slow running, for timed periods. In a typical fartlek session I jog for five minutes, and when the stopwatch beeps I switch over to a minute of fairly fast running: not a flat-out sprint, but at a much faster speed than a jog. When, another minute later, the watch beeps again, I go back into a jog. Then, another minute later, I stride out again . . . and so on, for as long as Bruce has decided: that usually means about eight efforts.

When Bruce can't be there – for instance, when I go away in winter to do some warm-weather training – he always provides me with a daily chart of everything he thinks I should carry out in his absence. I follow his guidelines, but not slavishly.

51

If for example, there's something I'm not happy with, for whatever reason, I can always phone him to talk about it. Then he'll say something along the lines, 'Well, you could do another 200 metres, if you like,' or, 'Why not drop that for today.' He never gives orders; he just responds to how I'm feeling, and gently suggests alternatives or improvements.

He has a similar influence on my weight training, which is not a major part of my overall training but which is nonetheless important. Bruce doesn't actually take part in these sessions, although he has seen me do them and he sets the exercises. As always, it's up to me to say, 'Right, I'm ready to increase the weight' (or keep it the same, or reduce it, or whatever the case might be). If I have a question, such as 'Should I take it over sixty kilos?' Bruce will say yes or no. He's always there when I need him.

Recently, I had a cold, and by the time the end of the week came I had missed some of my sessions. I rang up Bruce and said, 'I've missed three sessions. I've got three to do but obviously I can't manage all of them. Which one should I do?'

After a moment's thought he gently suggested the remedy. It was something which in a sense I had known all along, but I was glad to hear it from the horse's mouth.

Of course, if I cheat on training I'm cheating on myself and the whole point of everything is lost. Some of the training is tough, especially in bad weather during a British winter. Hill training can be hard to do on a regular basis. Sometimes I wake up in the morning, and look out of the window . . . and see the rain pouring down . . . I know I have to jog across to the local hill where I train, go up to the top and down to the bottom eighteen times (ninety metres, ascending or descending), then jog back afterwards. The temptation to stay under the bedclothes can be dreadfully strong.

Anyone who sees me working with Bruce is always

surprised at how little seems to pass between us. Sometimes he will call out the time I have just clocked for
one of the distances right when I'm preparing for the
next . . . But this is only for information; it's not that
he's trying to make me train harder. With this kind of
information I know whether I should pick up the pace
a bit, or slow down a little, depending on how things
are going.

In a typical training session, Bruce might very well say
only a few words – something along the lines: 'OK, you've
run such and such a time.' And I will take this in, then
reply: 'I wanted to run a second faster' (or a hundredth
faster, or whatever). He will listen, and we'll start walking
back to where I've left my kit, and that will be the end
of it. Somehow with just a couple of sentences or so,
we have communicated what each of us thinks about my
performance on that occasion . . . and the next time we're
working together this will be taken into account.

Another example of this chemistry between us occurred
while I was training in Florida, in early 1994. I was working
through a certain series of recoveries: six runs of 300 metres,
with short breaks between them. Bruce wandered up just as
I was finishing the fifth.

He said, 'You know, Sally, you're nearly ready to do eight
of these.'

I replied straight away, without thinking, 'Oh, all right
then; I'll do seven today!'

The entire exchange was over in a few seconds, and for
both of us it had happened spontaneously. The point is
that, without consciously realizing it, I had become ready
to increase the exercise, and, without Bruce consciously
realizing it, he had known that I was ready. With a minimum
of haggling we agreed what to do next.

I don't want to mystify this process, because in reality it

is a case of two people who, having grown to know and understand each other extremely well, now work in close harmony. Bruce never tells me that I've been going too slow or too fast, because he knows that all athletes have off days and good days. He still occasionally comes up with his famous quiet advice, 'Run tall, Sally.' (It always has its effect on me.) Or he'll say, 'Relax a bit more,' or, 'Think of your arms a bit more.'

When the session is finished Bruce usually comes to my side and then we'll walk back together. Into his silence I'll drop a comment – 'I think I went off a bit too hard,' or 'I should have worked a bit longer on that,' or something similar, in low-key manner. He will grunt quietly, and I'll know he concurs.

Bruce has won my total trust and respect, but it has to be said that he does demand a hell of a lot from his athletes. There are many who haven't stuck with him. A recent example is my friend (and roommate at big competitions) Jennifer Stoute. She trained for two years with Bruce, but in 1993 they came to a parting of the ways. As far as I know there was no great falling-out – just an acknowledgement that the special chemistry they both wanted was simply not there. Now Jennifer is training with another coach, but she and Bruce are still on friendly terms.

He works on the basis of no lavish praise and no big downers. You don't get him saying 'Well done' very often, but by the same token neither do you get 'That was terrible'. Even so, you know when you have done well. He will say, 'That was pretty good.' But it's not that often! I respect this, because I would not like someone who said it every time. Once, last winter, I actually heard him utter the words, 'That's probably one of the best sessions you've ever done.' I knew then I must have done well.

We have now reached a point where I can train for long

periods without him, but occasionally we will do intense courses together for about ten days. During this period he will see every session I do. From these he will know how I have been getting on during the rest of the year, and whether I have been training correctly for the last couple of months.

Another guide is my track sessions. He says that when these are going well I must be training hard and effectively in the other sessions I take on.

If anything terrible were to happen, and Bruce was no longer around, rather than starting again with someone else I would probably end up training myself. Perhaps from everything I have said about his methods it sounds as if I already do. In practical terms I know all the sessions that have to be done, and in many ways I know and can anticipate what he will say and advise in reaction to them. In this sense I don't 'need' him. All in all, though, I depend utterly on his quiet support and advice.

I had an unwelcome foretaste of life without Bruce in September 1984, when he changed jobs and moved to Oslo to work with the Norwegian Athletics Federation. Like the other members of the group I was devastated by the news, but unlike most of them I was determined to do something about it. The group, as a group, quickly fell apart, with everyone moving off to find other coaches, but I decided to stay with him.

By that time I had started my first job and had a little money coming in, and with the help of my parents, I was able to go across and stay in Bruce's house for short visits, and catch up on training.

The situation for Norwegian athletes is very different from the one in Britain: Oslo alone has three indoor tracks, and in general the Norwegian Federation treats its athletes almost too well. By British standards they are positively pampered! The training facilities are superb. On my first visit, in November, there wasn't much snow on the ground, so I was able to train in the open air. Even when the weather was colder, tracks with under-surface heating were readily available.

Bruce was already working with a new group of young athletes by the time I got there, so I would do my sessions, joining in with the others. Also, as Sue, his wife, was still training at the time, I joined in with her for circuit training, with some running afterwards. On other nights Sue would stay at home and Bruce and I would do a track session at the Sports Institute.

Maintaining the continuity of his training meant I had to go to a lot more trouble, of course, but I have never been sorry about it. In the end, Bruce returned from Norway in 1988, and he's now back with the British Athletics Federation, as a national coach. (There was another period when he worked elsewhere – in Wetherby, Yorkshire; I duly followed him there for long weekends.)

So at this point I have been with him for fourteen years, and we have an awful lot of trust in each other. He's not exactly a father-figure to me (and I'm not exactly a daughter-figure to him), but there are elements of that bond in our relationship. He's brought me along over the years, guided me and nurtured my ability. Sometimes he can be possessive about me, but I understand all that.

Naturally, we've had our ups and downs. If he's upset he'll keep it in, but I can usually tell when there's something wrong. When I was a Junior he hated it whenever I went off somewhere – say, to one of the national coaching weekends; these were to me great fun, but Bruce, I think, saw them as an opportunity for some other coach to influence me. I enjoyed the social aspect of trips like that – the whole

Aged nine months in the garden of our house.

When I was two, playing with a ball and our family dog.

On my scooter at Old Farm, aged two.

Even at the age of six I loved racing.

I received the prize for winning the obstacle race, also when I was six.

In Mrs Gordon's class at Chigwell Primary when I was 11.

When I was 12 – the Essex Ladies Athletic Club.

Competing in the long jump in the Club Championships, aged 12.

And in the Southern League 75m hurdles aged 13.

This was taken at Old Farm in 1985. Dad had told Jon as a joke that he could ride a cow . . . and Jon had believed him!

The under-20s England Team to Australia, 1985. Jon is standing next to me in the back row. We met on this trip.

After winning the 100m hurdles at the 1986 Commonwealth Games in Edinburgh.

Receiving my first major gold medal at the Commonwealth Games in 1986. Wendy Jeal won silver and Glynis Nunn bronze.

Seeing my name on the electronic scoreboard was a proud moment for my family and me.

Undergoing knee massage during training for the Essex Ladies Club's inclusion in the European Club Championships, Portugal, 1986.

Hurdling during the Championships, Portugal, 1986.

Hurdling in the city in front of my work-mates at Ball, Baker and Leake after the 1986 Commonwealth Games.

With room-mates Kim Hagger, Joanne Mulliner and Sally-Anne Short at the Seoul Olympics, 1988. This was the closing ceremony and we were having a great time.

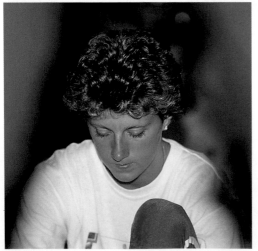

This was taken just after I hit the eighth hurdle in the 400m race at the Pescara Grand Prix, 1989 – I'd fallen and was not happy.

business of a large group of young people hanging out together for a weekend – but many times Bruce didn't want me to go.

In the winter of 1985 I was selected to go on a Junior International trip to Australia and New Zealand, and I was expecting to meet resistance from him. In the event he was great about that . . . especially considering the importance of what was to happen to me on that trip.

If I were asked to evaluate what Bruce has done for me, to try to quantify it, I would say without a pause for thought that I owe him a great deal. I said this to him once, and he drily pointed out that I do some of it for myself.

'Well,' I replied, 'it's one hundred per cent, then, of everything that comes from outside me.' We argued cheerfully a bit longer, and in the end agreed on a figure that was somewhat lower.

In fact, although no athlete could produce top results without working with a coach, other factors do come into it.

For instance, every athlete makes good use of physiotherapists, without whom many a highly trained body would surely come to grief. Recently, I have been talking to a nutritionist, who has been helping me plan my diet for the peak of the season. And of course Jon, my husband, has been a fantastic source of support, in all sorts of ways.

But the coach remains fundamental. As I have tried to show here, Bruce has shaped and inspired me for years. Above all, I have learned from him a vital thing that gives me a definite edge over my competitors. He has taught me to focus on a race, and think my way through to winning it. How this works is best explained by describing how it works in practice, so I hope it will become clear later in this book.

Chapter 5

Pentathlete to Hurdler

In 1984, when I left school, I was faced with a particular dilemma, one that few other people of my age come up against. I felt I had to choose between a job and athletics, the reason being that each one would occupy most of my time, and either would exclude the other. I already knew how much of my week was spent on training, and it was difficult to conceive of any job that would fit alongside.

In my last year at school I had learned shorthand and typing, and so I decided, as a short-term measure, to look for work as a secretarial temp. I signed on with an agency, and told them the ideal for me would be to work odd days here and there. They came up with a few placements, but there obviously wasn't a lot of work around that was suitable for me, so I got a job in a bar in High Beach, not far from my parents' farm (I was of course still living at home, being incapable of supporting myself financially). I worked at the pub at lunchtimes and for a couple of evenings every week. I liked the extra money, but I didn't particularly enjoy the work.

Then, out of the blue, the temping agency came up with a completely different kind of job. They knew of a lady who was expecting her second baby, and she wanted someone to come and play with her first child, a little boy. It would only be for one week. I had never done anything like that, but because I had always liked children I thought I would give it a try. I went along, hit it off straight away with both the little boy and the mother, and at the end of the week she offered me the job on a permanent basis.

The family soon knew all about my running, and we worked out a schedule to suit us all. From Monday to Thursday every week I started at 9.00 a.m. and continued until 4.00 p.m., with occasional evenings for babysitting. I really enjoyed all this. The two little boys, Ben and Alex, were lovely kids and I became very attached to them. I used to get their breakfast and lunch, do any ironing, vacuuming and cleaning that was necessary, and in the afternoons I would take them out for a walk. I'm proud of my years as a nanny!

All good things come to an end, and in 1986 a friend of Bruce's mentioned his accountants in London, a firm called Ball Baker Leake. He approached them on my behalf to see if they could offer me a part-time job, with the usual proviso that I would need to take time off regularly for training. Apparently they made discreet enquiries to see if I had any athletic talent. I had just that year won at the Commonwealth Games, so I think they realized I showed some promise!

They offered me a job for three days a week, 10.00 a.m. to 4.00 p.m., at their offices in Essex Street, close to the Victoria Embankment. I started off in the post room and filing department; part of my arrangement with them allowed me to go away for up to three weeks at a time, so the work had to be the kind where I could leave the job behind me without inconveniencing everyone else. I also had a free pass to Cannon's Gym in the City, so I would spend most lunchtimes using their equipment. I'd leave work at four o'clock, be home by five, then do my training in the evenings.

In 1989 Ball Baker Leake merged with a larger firm of accountants called Pannell Kerr Forster, whose offices were in Hatton Garden. Although I was at first a little uncertain whether any new arrangements would suit me, I found my situation actually improved.

PKF turned out to be a most enlightened firm. They offered me the chance of reducing my attendance to only two days a week, and in addition allowed me to work on a flexitime basis. By this time I had run in the final at the Seoul Olympics, so they could see where my athletics career was heading. I was promoted to PKF's Research Department, where, although my work continued to be the sort I could temporarily set aside from time to time, it was noticeably more interesting. I was checking share prices for the day, and company information, and so on.

Broadly speaking, PKF allowed me all the time off work I wanted, and with a reasonable amount of notice I could change my days around. In addition, they paid me a fixed yearly salary. It was obviously not as large as a full-time one, but I was just about able to live off it. I realized from the beginning that I had been really lucky to get this arrangement. Very few athletes have jobs that dovetail so conveniently.

In 1991, when I was starting to train hard for the Barcelona Olympics the following year, they allowed me to reduce my time at the office to one day a week, which was marvellous. But after that, when I came home from Barcelona with the gold medal, everything changed. I was suddenly so busy that working even one day a week for them became impossible.

I'm still associated with PKF now, although I don't go in to work for them any more. They use my name on their company letterheads. In a very real sense they were my first major sponsors, and I owe them more than I can say.

I was lucky in finding all these jobs, because a lot of athletes have to go on the dole. Quite apart from all the aggravations that go with signing on, the dole is not the answer. Being unemployed leaves you with too much time to think about your training and your athletics. I return briefly to my point that an athletics career is followed best when it is part of a larger, more ordinary life, with daily concerns. For example, if you're on the dole and you suffer an injury, what do you do then? If I had been injured during this period, at least I could have gone back to work and thrown myself into that.

It is a serious lack in our country that there aren't a few more employers like PKF. I just hope younger athletes coming up behind me will be as fortunate as I was.

These working arrangements were the background to my early athletic career. In a sense, my adult sporting career began at roughly the same time as I left school, because it was in the summer of 1984, when I was seventeen coming up to eighteen, that I made my first attempt to qualify for the British Olympic Team. I very much wanted to go to Los Angeles.

I had gone through my last years at school as first a pentathlete, then since 1983 as a heptathlete. By far my best event in the heptathlon was the 100m hurdles, and so I set out to try to qualify in that as a separate event also. What followed taught me something of a lesson in the way these things are managed.

It began in June of that year, with the UK Championships. It is widely accepted that you have to do well in these to be able to go forward to the Olympic Trials in July. For technical reasons I couldn't compete in the 100m hurdles as a separate event; I had to concentrate my efforts in the 100m hurdles race within the heptathlon. I did really well in this, and logged the third fastest time of all those taking part, including the girls who weren't in the heptathlon. The rules say that the first three over the line go on to the Trials, but I was passed over in this event. Very galling!

And in the heptathlon itself I came up against another technicality. The score in this event is calculated as a number of points, aggregated from the results in all seven of the individual components. As I was better in some of the events than others, getting a high points score was always a bit of a problem for me, but that year I did reasonably well. I scored 5,553, which put me above the minimum set by the Olympics Committee: 5,550 points. Unfortunately, the British Olympics officials had set their minimum at 5,560!

So in spite of the fact that I had come second in the heptathlon, and in effect third in the 100m hurdles, I was not selected for the Olympic Team. Another girl, Sharon Danville, was selected instead, even though I had beaten her many times in the past.

Since then, the official thinking about Team selection has changed slightly, and now they like to be sure that several of the best young athletes can go to the Olympics. In this they reflect Bruce's belief, and now mine too, that before you can hope to pick up an Olympic medal you must have some previous experience of competing in the Games. If they had thought like this in 1984, instead of rejecting me, in effect, for being 'only seventeen', I would probably have gone to Los Angeles.

Bruce and I were both disappointed by the outcome, he more than I was. At the beginning of that year I certainly had not seen myself as a possible Olympic contender. It was just that I had had a really good year, and during that time, as I got better, I felt the wish to go to the Olympics growing in me.

Afterwards, I made a resolution that I would never let that happen again, never let myself get into a position where I might not be selected. I always want to be sure of that place if I decide to go after it.

However, from this disappointment grew an idea that was eventually to change the direction of my career. As I sat quietly with Bruce, talking over what had happened, he said, 'You know, it might be worth having a go at concentrating on only one event.'

I said, 'Then it has to be sprint hurdles.'

'If you say so, Sally.'

Once the decision had been made, the heptathlon lifted off me like an old weight that had been holding me down. No more javelin and shot. Best of all, no more high jump!

Bruce always said I was a natural hurdler, but not only did he teach me well I was surrounded by other athletes who were good at hurdling. I used to like watching them to see how they did it.

I competed in the sprint hurdles for the rest of the 1984 season, and by the end of it I had established two landmarks that meant a great deal to me.

I was number 1 *in the world* for women of my age (I was only just eighteen). And I held the British Junior Record for the 100m hurdles, at 13.30 seconds. Ten years later, that record is still mine.

When 1984 turned into 1985, something happened at the beginning of the new year that would eventually turn out to be even more influential than dropping the heptathlon. Together with a large group of other young athletes, I left England for a winter tour of Australia and New Zealand.

Chapter 6

Australia and
New Zealand, 1985

As you settle into an athletic career, you realize that each year follows roughly the same pattern as all the others. The season begins at the end of May and finishes in mid-September. There then follows a break, a short but complete break in which you do anything on earth *except* train or compete. In November you start training again, getting ready for the following year's season. You train through the dark winter months, compete briefly in the short indoor season (February and March), then continue training until the main season begins.

To go off to Australia in January, the time when the summer competitive season is in full swing there, can completely disrupt this pattern.

A Junior England International team was being put together for a three-week tour of the Antipodes, and for me it would be my first chance to go on a real trip abroad. When Bruce raised no serious objections I signed up for the trip with great eagerness. The way it was presented to me was that everyone knew, because of the time of year, that none of us was going to be on top form. The racing was not expected to be the highlight of the whole trip. The main purpose was to make it into a 'friendly': we would go over there, enjoy ourselves, and hope to race as well as possible. It was designed as a learning experience: to go and compete against other countries, meet other athletes on a social basis, get acclimatized to competing in a different part of the world. It started to feel irresistible.

Two athletes were selected for each event, and off we went.

I remember noticing Jon Bigg on the aircraft on the outward flight: he was one of only two guys wearing shorts – everyone else had a tracksuit on – and he walked around, smiled a lot and seemed to know many people. I knew I had seen him before, during one of our weekend get-togethers up in Gateshead, maybe a year or two earlier. He had been one of the team. I don't remember much about him from the weekend itself, but on the train on the way back I had been sitting with a group of people and he came along the aisle. Then, as on the plane, he seemed friendly and self-confident, grinning at everyone. I thought then, 'Oh he's quite nice!'

Flying out to Australia I suddenly thought the same thing.

When we arrived in Melbourne we went to the university, where we going to be staying during the first part of the trip. All of a sudden Jon was always around, part of the group, chatting away. I hit it off with him from the word go. He was so easy to get on with, and he blended in with us all as if he were a friend we had known for years. I remember sitting quite close to him during dinner in the immense dining hall in the university, and afterwards, during the rest of the three-week trip, we were usually together, hanging out in a loosely defined group of about half a dozen of us. Some days we would go down to the beach, or we would train together, or we would go swimming; sometimes it was the whole group, and at other times it would be just the two of us. Nothing binding was said or expected; no commitments were made.

Yes, I definitely fancied him, but I wasn't about to rush into anything. We were just getting to know each other. This set a pattern that was to continue for several more months: we spent much of the time taking the mickey out of one another, rather than chatting each other up.

We stayed for about a week in Melbourne, where we had just one competition, then we went to Brisbane for another. From there we flew to New Zealand, where we had one meet planned in Auckland and another in Christchurch. That was the three weeks. It turned out to feel more like a holiday than an arduous tour. There were whole days when we did nothing more strenuous than sit around on a beach, drinking and chatting.

Gradually, Jon and I grew a little closer. While we were in Melbourne and Brisbane none of us were forming couples, but by the time we got to Auckland it seemed only natural to be together for much of the time, and Jon and I would find ourselves on our own more and more often.

While we were still in Auckland, on the second-to-last night of the whole tour, one of those little incidents that inevitably make you much closer happened to us.

Jon was staying in the dormitory used by the men, and he had a tiny cell-like room. It was midsummer, the dormitories obviously hadn't been in use for some time, and all the windows were tightly closed. His room was really stuffy. We were going to see the movie *Gremlins* that evening, and before we went out Jon opened the window for some fresh air.

When we returned Jon went up to his room and, I

gather, fell asleep immediately. He was woken up, about an hour later, by something making *zzzz! zzzz!* noises. He reached over and turned on the light. The room was full of mosquitoes, and already his face was covered in bites.

He knew he had to get out of there, so he took his sheet and went and lay down in the common room. A few minutes later he changed his mind: he realized that the other guys would discover him there in the morning, and if that happened he was likely to be woken up by a bucketful of cold water thrown over him, or find he had no clothes on, or some such thing.

The first I knew about all this was a few minutes later. It was the middle of the night, the room was dark, and I was woken up by someone tapping on the door.

'Who is it?' I asked.

Jon said, 'I'm being bitten to pieces . . . Can I sleep on your floor?'

I opened the door, and there he was with all these insect bites on his face! He came in, and after we had chatted for a bit he lay down on the floor and we tried to get back to sleep. We drifted off in the end.

The next thing either of us knew was that it was morning, and someone else was knocking on the door!

The point was that we were not children but the tour managers had made it pretty clear we weren't supposed to go into each other's dormitories at night. One of them must have seen Jon coming across from the men's wing. What should we do? There was just one place to hide Jon, and that was in the wardrobe! He dived in, clutching the sheet around his waist.

Before he was completely out of sight, there was another knock. I got to the door and eased it open, my heart in my mouth . . . but it was only Joanne Mulliner. She breezed in, glad to see I was awake, and ready for a chat. I closed the door to the corridor, and Jon came out of the wardrobe looking more than a little embarrassed.

To this day I don't think Joanne believes that it was an entirely innocent episode.

We went to the airport two days later and boarded the plane for the interminable flight home. Now Jon and I were feeling close, and we sat next to each other all the way. We were in the central block of seats, where there are four across, and I remember that, because we had these to ourselves, when we slept I spread out on the seats and he slept on the floor below me.

At Heathrow, we introduced each other to our respective parents. Then, inevitably, and extremely reluctantly, we said goodbye.

I had not had many serious boyfriends before Jon came along. I think the longest of these relationships had lasted only six months or so. Although I was interested in meeting potential boyfriends, I came across very few who understood how much my training could clash with a social life. Many athletes marry other athletes for just this reason. They have no need to explain or to make excuses about their commitment to training.

Of course, you never spell these things out to yourself until the right person comes along, and then you no longer have to.

From the day we returned from New Zealand, Jon and I slipped into a happy relationship that has grown slowly ever since. There was a slight blip a few days later, because I had already arranged to go to Portugal on a training trip, but we exchanged 'anonymous' Valentine cards before I left, and as soon as I was back we were instantly in touch again.

Jon had earned his first Senior International vest for an indoor event against the USA, and had returned on Sunday after the race the evening before. I came in from Portugal on the same day. Driving home, he suddenly got it into his head to drop in on me. He wasn't quite sure what time I was going to be back, so he went to a Little Chef restaurant on the main road near the farm, and sat in the window waiting to see if we would go past. Somehow or other he managed to spot Dad's car! He gave us twenty minutes to unload all my stuff from the car, then turned up at the house, as if by chance.

This weekend visit was the first of many that were to follow, on and off, for the next two years. Jon stayed at the farm that night, set his travel alarm and got up at 5.00 a.m. He had to be at work in Brighton by 9.00 a.m. (At this time he was working for Steve Ovett's sports-clothes company, although this job only continued into the summer that year.) He says now that he did so much travelling to and fro that the tolls he had to pay for using the Dartford Tunnel singlehandedly built the Queen Elizabeth Bridge.

At the same time, we were both fattening British Telecom's coffers.

My life started to change once I met Jon and his family, and began to spend more time with them in Brighton. I had always been happy on the farm, but this was different. Life was opening up around me.

Like my parents, both of Jon's had been athletes when they were younger. His father now worked for a publishing company, and this was where Jon went to work for a while, after he left Steve Ovett's business, although there was a period between when he was on the dole. At this time he lived at my parents' farm during the week. This was when I was still working as a part-time nanny.

We spent as much time together as possible, either in Essex or in Brighton. I remember the very first time I went down to

Brighton, because I had to borrow my Dad's car. I'm not sure what happened, but I think I must have been driving fast and I arrived earlier than planned. Thinking Jon would be there, I simply knocked on the door and was invited inside. In fact, not only was Jon not there, no one was sure when he would be back. Meanwhile, I tried to make conversation with his mother, whom I'd met briefly, and the other two people who were there. One was his brother, and the other was one of Jon's ex-girlfriends!

My first impression of Joyce and John, Jon's mum and dad, were how young and active they seemed. They made me feel so much at home. Maybe it was because they had had three sons but no daughter. I was the first girlfriend any of them had known who lived so far away she had to stay overnight.

And Jon's parents fitted so naturally into and around his athletics and training that they seemed like a team behind him. Gradually, as things moved forward in my own career, the team shifted around. Now Joyce has been my secretary for two years, and John sometimes comes down to time me when I'm training.

The first weekend I was there we went out with Jon's circle of friends. Again, they made me feel I was one of them. All this was rather different from my own life. Back in Chigwell I often went out for the evening with my brother and his friends. I'm not complaining about that, but I fitted in with Jon's Brighton crowd as if they were *my* friends, and had been all along. They totally changed me: they were arty, funny, articulate. They dressed interestingly. Within the first couple of weeks I had my hair cut short and switched to wearing black clothes. God knows what my parents thought! Whenever I had to go home I hated it; Jon and I would drive as far as Crawley, where we would have a tearful farewell. Then I would ring him up as soon as I got home.

We had our first Christmas together that year, and immediately we ran into a problem familiar to most couples: how were we to divide the time spent with our respective families? We agonized for a while, until Jon pointed out that my mum and dad had started farming turkeys for the first time that year. They were obviously going to be busy right up to the last minute, and we didn't want to burden them with extra work on Christmas Day. So we decided to be in Brighton, and drive to the farm on Boxing Day.

I really got into the mood for a party, and Jon and his brothers started winding me up a little. They said we ought to put on fancy dress on Christmas Day. I thought that was a great idea, so without telling anyone I started work on a costume. I decided to be seasonal, and go as a turkey!

When the day came no one else seemed to be in any great rush to get into costume, so I started asking about it. I still didn't realize what was going on. After lunch, Jon's brother Matthew said, 'Come on, then. Let's go and get changed.'

I went up to my room and came down a few minutes later. I'd put on an old, laddered pair of cream-coloured tights, a pair of running shorts, and a white top which I'd covered all over with turkey feathers. I finished the effect with a swimming hat and a home-made beak.

I walked into the room, and only at this point did I realize I was the only one in costume. Jon's still got those photos, hidden away somewhere . . .

Jon was training with Steve Ovett before he worked for his clothes company, and this was the period when Ovett was breaking world records. When Jon and I first met he was doing a lot of heavy training with Steve. It was a major contrast with my own training. We were each surprised, and a little shocked, when we saw what the other was doing. It seemed to me that he was over-training.

To Jon? Well, once he said to me, semi-seriously, 'Is that

all you have to do to be number 1 hurdler in the country? You could do so much more!'

In a small degree the contrast between us arose from the difference in the length of our events. Jon ran middle-distance, concentrating on the 800 metres flat, and the training techniques are quite different.

But to a much larger degree the contrast sprang from my coach's philosophy about long-term training. Bruce was deliberately holding me back.

He once said that if I wanted I could become a brilliant Junior, perhaps the top in the country. After that, he said, I would burn out. He already had me in mind as an Olympic contender, and, as he said, Juniors don't win the Olympics. This came as something of a revelation to Jon, who has subsequently told me that seeing me being deliberately held back was one of the biggest lessons in life he had learned.

At the time, I felt Jon was being taken miles beyond the training he should have been doing. He was getting results, but I used to worry about injuries. I know this sounds as though I'm being wise after the event, as Jon was badly injured the following year, but one of the things Bruce has always drummed into me is that over-training makes you vulnerable to injury, especially when you're younger.

On the other hand, Jon's vigorous approach to training has been a tremendous boon to me at times. I think particularly of the winter of 1992/1993, following the Barcelona Olympics, when I was trying to keep training at the same time as all the fuss and bother in the media was going on.

We went away to Tallahassee in Florida for three weeks of warm-weather training, just the two of us. In spite of my best efforts, I really had not done as much work before Christmas as I should have. It meant that we had to cram the optimum amount of high-intensity work into the three weeks. There were mornings when I would wake up with a groan and say, 'I can't do it today.' And Jon would say, 'All right, but let's just do some jogging. See how you feel.'

So we would get out there and start a little jogging, and once I felt the air moving into my lungs, and my body loosening up, I would feel like going on and doing the rest. Once, I felt so disinclined to train that the only thing Jon could get me to agree to was a short walk; yet, once again, as soon as we started I felt a lot better.

I think probably the greatest help Jon has ever given me was during those three weeks. We trained hard, much harder than I would have done normally. It would be impossible for me to train like that, week in and week out, on a routine basis, because I would break down, get injured. But for a short, intensive period like that I can benefit from hard work.

That trip to Florida taught me a lot about motivation. The distractions still continue in England, and when I'm at home I do manage to keep up with all the training I should. But it's always an effort. I have to set time aside deliberately, keep a diary. If I'm able to get away for a special training trip abroad, I can put in an effort of 80–100 per cent every time. When I'm at home, I might have to be in London for a whole day, come home tired, then go out and do a training session; in circumstances like that I can only put in perhaps 60–70 per cent effort.

Because I realize how important it is to keep training, I'm having to keep a stricter control on what I do with my time. I had no idea how much disruption would follow my winning the Barcelona Olympics. I was rushing around all over the place, and trying to fit in training when I could. The difference now is that I set aside one day a week for publicity work, or for public appearances, and the rest of the week I'm at home. If the media want to interview me now, they come and see me.

Even so, being at home has other distractions. Although I'm always more relaxed there, of course, with my cats and my friends, I frequently have to dash out to do some shopping, or I must clean the house or make umpteen phone calls.

A trip abroad, especially to a country with a warm climate in winter, allows me to concentrate on training, and it gives me time to think about what I want to do. I try to work out exactly what I want to achieve during the summer, and how to go about it. In short, I build up my motivation for the season ahead.

In the 1988 Budget, Nigel Lawson, then Chancellor of the Exchequer, announced an extension of double tax-relief for couples who bought property together and completed the purchase before August that year. Jon and I had been going out together for about three and a half years, and it was obvious to one and all that we had become a permanent feature in each other's lives. That was also the time when everyone was saying you should get on the bottom rung of the housing ladder.

We managed to find a place and complete all the formalities just in time, and we exchanged contracts on my birthday, 29 July. Buying a home symbolized a little bit more of a commitment to each other while we remained unmarried, and it would also provide a stable background for us, after all the travelling to and fro. By this time I was starting to earn a little money from running, and Jon was working in London.

It was just an ordinary one-bedroomed flat on the second floor of a Victorian semi in Brighton. There were four other flats in the house. The main problem with ours was that it needed a lot of repairs and redecoration before it would be how we wanted it. At this time I was working Tuesdays and

Thursdays at PKF. I would go up to London on a Tuesday morning, stay the night with my parents on Tuesday and Wednesday, then return to Brighton after I finished work on Thursday.

We had agreed that we would not live at the flat until we had finished the decorating. I was due to go to Seoul in September, and would be away for five weeks.

When I had gone, Jon set to work. He apparently began by pulling out the entire contents of the kitchen, and in the process wrecked the place. I was spared much of the mess, but he told me afterwards that the one thing he had not allowed for in his scheme was any time for sleep! He had forgotten that the Olympics were being broadcast on British TV during the wee small hours. He would be up all night watching the Olympics, then get on the train and go to work in London. When he returned in the evening he went straight to the flat, did some of the decorating, then watched the Olympics all night again. The only rest he was getting was on the trains going to and from London.

I came back from Seoul bubbling over with excitement, and found Jon in a state of imminent physical collapse.

That same day, while I was still fresh off the plane from Korea, we went out and bought a bed. Then we moved in.

Chapter 7

Commonwealth Gold, 1986

The period of eighteen months between February 1985, when we returned from New Zealand, and July 1986, when I ran in the Commonwealth Games, was one in which Jon and I felt our individual careers were going off in different directions.

Jon seemed to flourish in the 1985 season. Ten days after we got back he ran in the National Cross-Country and came about fiftieth. I know he was really pleased with this, because it was a brilliant placing for someone who normally ran middle distance. A week after that he achieved his first Indoor International at 800 metres, and came second.

Success in sport is often relative, dependent on the particular circumstances. That year Jon's results were allied to the fact that young athletes are banded into age groups. The year before, Jon had been competing at the Intermediate level and was one of the oldest boys in that group. In 1985 he graduated to the Senior level and instantly found himself, an eighteen-year-old, competing against much older men at the peak of their careers. Of course, all athletes have to contend with the transition, but this was Jon's year for it and he was doing well under the circumstances.

Meanwhile, my own career seemed to have levelled out. Again, it was strictly relative. I still competed widely, and I won a lot of races, but I didn't feel I was progressing. It was as if I had lost the curving acceleration of the early years, and now although I was still moving forward it was only with momentum from the past.

I try never to make excuses for myself, but, now that several years have passed, hindsight offers some explanations.

I believe the disappointment about the Los Angeles Olympics ran much deeper than I realized at the time, and that it was still trickling through my mind. It was a discouraging memory I had to carry around with me.

Like Jon, I had just moved up into Senior grade, and was competing against older, more developed athletes.

Another factor was that 1984 had been a real landmark year for me, and quite possibly I was feeling a little let down by the discovery that not every succeeding year was going to be so rewarding. I had improved so much in 1984. In June I had set the British Junior Record at Crystal Palace, with a time of 13.30 seconds. This wasn't a flash in the pan, because over a number of races I had been bringing my personal best down from 13.54 seconds. So in 1985 I had expected that progress to continue. I was hoping to get my personal best down to 13.20 seconds or so, but in spite of my best efforts it stayed at about 13.30 seconds and 13.40 seconds.

Finally, I do believe that in training terms the trip to Australia and New Zealand had been harmful. There were the three weeks lost while we were away, followed by the week afterwards when I had jet lag and wasn't feeling at my best. That's effectively a month lost, in the most crucial part of the training cycle.

Although I went to Portugal for training in February, and

to Paris in April, I don't think I really caught up. But I must keep this in perspective. I don't think I at any point said, 'Something's wrong with me. What's happening?'

Jon, though, riding his own high, did not see it in exactly those terms. Because by this time Bruce was in Norway, and I was frequently visiting Brighton, it was only natural that Jon and I would train together a lot of the time.

Jon told me once, 'You've got the attack and the motivation. You've got the ability to do what you want to achieve.'

'But I always feel so inadequate,' I said. 'I feel as if I don't do enough. You and your group always seem to be training so hard.'

It was the familiar difference again, although I was glad and grateful for his confidence in me. He went with me to Norway on a couple of occasions, and trained with Bruce.

There were no wintertime distractions or interruptions to the training schedule when 1986 arrived, but once again my career and Jon's were destined to diverge. He had been training hard, and it looked as if he would continue the momentum he had set up the previous summer.

But something went wrong. It was almost as if, having brought himself to a peak of training perfection, he was scared to put it to the test. His results were way below the level we both knew would reflect his true capabilities.

Perhaps only I, of all the people around him, could sense his frustration and disappointment. After a couple of races he quickly came to terms with the fact that he wasn't achieving anything like what he should, but it didn't help his deep sense of disappointment. He had recently left work and was on the dole, and whenever he spoke about what was going on he did so in terms of having put so much effort into athletics, and now that was proving to be dicey.

For a time I wondered whether all this signalled the end of

our relationship. He just didn't seem to be the same person. I understood his problem was that he couldn't run on the track but did not really know why. In the end he went for a long visit to California; it seemed that he wanted to stay away from athletics, and not talk about it at all.

Even so, Jon is not a quitter, and when he came back from the US he had worked his way through the crisis. The following winter he went back into training, and I knew then that his normal optimism was returning.

Meanwhile, my own year was turning out to be an unusual one: 1986 had some surprises lying in wait for me.

Because I had gone through an uninterrupted winter of training, I went into the 1986 season feeling good. The big event on the immediate horizon was the Commonwealth Games, to be held in Edinburgh and beginning at the end of July. If I wanted to go to these, and represent England, I had some hard work to do first. I was not seriously thought of as a contender as the season began. England's number 1 sprint hurdler was Shirley Strong, and number 2 was Lesley-Ann Skeete. I was number 3, but it seemed unlikely I would be picked.

In the second week of June I ran for Essex Ladies in the European Clubs Championships, and set a time of 13.52 seconds; it was nowhere near my personal best, but it made me feel I was getting into gear.

Two big competitions then came one after the other in quick order: the UK Championships and the WAAA (Women's Amateur Athletics Association) Championships. I won the sprint hurdles in both of these – beating Lesley-Ann and Shirley – and in the WAAA I set a new personal best of 13.13 seconds. I felt that at last I was getting back into the groove I had slipped out of in 1985.

The immediate effect of these wins was twofold. Firstly, I

was promoted to the coveted position of number 1 women's sprint hurdler in Britain, and secondly I was given a place in the Commonwealth Games.

From a racing technique point of view, I had won both of these races with a late recovery. In the UK Championships I was in second place at the last hurdle, and snatched the win in the run-in to the finishing line; in the WAAA race I had been in fourth position halfway through the race, and had made up all that lost ground in the last fifty metres.

It was almost as if, even then, I was telling myself I might do better with a longer distance to run.

The 1986 Commonwealth Games coincided with my twentieth birthday, and my heat was scheduled for 31 July, two days after. I scored a good time in the heat, and went into the final the next day feeling very relaxed and confident. By this time Shirley Strong, recovering from an injury, was not a contender, so my main rivals were Lesley-Ann and another British hurdler, Wendy Jeal.

I won the gold with a time of 13.29 seconds, leaving Wendy Jeal quite a distance behind me (she ran 13.41 seconds). The bronze medal went to the Australian athlete Glynis Nunn.

It was my first gold for England! My first major championship!

I headed for Stuttgart and the European Championships with high hopes.

They call the Commonwealth Games the friendly games; compared with many other big meets they are small, almost intimate. The European Games, by contrast, are on a massive scale.

Built also on the grand scale was the world record holder, a beefy-looking Bulgarian called Yordanka Donkova. All through the summer this formidable athlete had been trimming hundredths of a second off the world record: in July she had set it at 12.40 seconds, but by the week before the beginning of the European Championships she had got this down, race by race, to 12.29 seconds! (She has since trimmed it even further, to 12.21 seconds.) It was my misfortune in the heat to be put in the next lane to hers.

As we settled down on the starting blocks, I suddenly noticed her hands. They were mutilated: the tips of two of the fingers on each hand were missing. I imagined a dreadful accident, involving some kind of industrial implement in a distant Iron Curtain country. She grunted as she settled on the blocks, a great and terrifying champion beside me.

I was at the beginning of a race! I was thinking about the woman next to me! My concentration had gone!

I came a dismal sixth at 13.22 seconds, and was out of the event.

Later, Wendy Jeal qualified in her heat, and went through to the semifinal.

For the first time in my career, I had allowed another runner to psych me out, break my concentration. I swore that it would be the last time I let anyone do that to me.

The next morning, Bruce took me to the warm-up track. He knew I had been crying. He knew how I felt, in every subtle degree. I blamed myself, not for running badly but for letting my attention wander. He also knew that I would not let it happen again. As we went out on to the track I wondered what he was going to do.

While I warmed up I saw him putting out some hurdles.

'We're going to do something totally different,' he said. 'Here you are, here's the next challenge. Just go and run.'

They were low hurdles, at the spacing for 400 metres.

*   *   *

The 1986 season was almost at an end, but when I started training for 1987 I had two events to think about. As I have already pointed out, most of the time I spend on training goes on building up strength, fitness and speed, with hurdling technique only coming in towards the end. Although there *are* differences in physical requirements – the sprint hurdles require 'burst' energy, while the 400m hurdles are more of a sustained effort – I did not have to make any fundamental changes to the way I trained.

When the 1987 season began I was still treated, and I still thought of myself, as a 100m hurdler. In fact, I was ranked British number 1 in this event, and therefore in every way I thought of it as my main event. Through that summer I ran 13.01 seconds five times. If I was stuck in a groove, at least it was a fast one!

Another big plus in my life was Bruce's return. His three-year contract with the Norwegians had ended, and he was back in Britain.

Then came the World Championships in Rome, close to the end of the season. Although I qualified in my heat for the 100m hurdles, I came sixth in the semifinals and was out of the competition.

The following week I ran my first-ever 400m hurdles. It was an experimental race, for Essex Ladies. I came in at 59.90 seconds, which, though not brilliant (the British record at that time was 56.04 seconds), was a time I felt happy with. I was good at hurdling, and I had always been a strong runner with a good finish. Maybe this distance would suit me better?

During the winter, Bruce and I conducted a post-mortem for the season just finished, and at last I faced up to some hard truths.

I held the Commonwealth gold, it was true, and I could beat anyone in Britain in the sprint hurdles . . . but some uncomfortable facts surrounded these achievements. One was that there had been a boycott of the Commonwealth Games by the African countries, so I had not been tried against every Commonwealth athlete in the event. Following this, on my next two international outings, the European and the World, I had not done at all well.

Bruce summed it up. 'There are ladies from the East European countries you are going to chase forever,' he said. 'Let's not ask why. Let's change to 400m hurdles.'

Chapter 8

Sprint Hurdler to 400 Metres Hurdler

Four long years lay between the Olympics in Seoul and Barcelona, but I saw that time as a necessary period of preparation. I was now firmly targeting the 1992 Olympics as the event I most wanted to win.

In my wider life, I had at last arrived at a permanent living arrangement with the man I loved, I was gradually gaining recognition as an athlete, I was able to make a reasonable amount of money from athletics (although my part-time job with PKF continued), and in general I was beginning to live life to the full.

There was one cloud on my personal horizon, however. This was that in 1987 Jon had been injured in a race. After his trip to California he trained hard and ran well throughout the following season, setting several personal bests. He came third in the Southern Counties, and in one race even beat Steve Ovett. The week after that he ran an Inter-Counties Representative match in Corby, and was accidentally spiked by another runner. His Achilles tendon was punctured, but not, fortunately, torn. The injury incapacitated him, though, and was sufficient to put him out of competitive running for about four years.

For me, the athletics seasons between the two Olympics had their successes and failures, but overall it was a time of steadily growing athletic ability.

By the end of 1988 I had the satisfaction of a good Olympic début behind me, and I held a number of records.

I genuinely believe that few athletes are motivated solely by the desire to win and hold records, but that most of us see a record as something that adds a little extra to the thrill of a big win. Having said this, I know that a record time (or distance) is a way of measuring someone's career as it develops. My own first record was an English Schools record for the long jump, in 1980. Although that is now far in my past, I will never forget the day I won it, nor how exciting it felt at the time.

In 1988 I won records in three different events. The first of the year was in Budapest, when I won the European Indoor Championships 400m flat, in a time of 51.77 seconds. This was a British Indoor record, and it still stands.

The same is true of my time of 12.82 seconds for the 100m hurdles, which I won in Zürich during the summer. With this I beat Shirley Strong's British record, which had stood unchallenged for five years. Then there was the British record I established in the Seoul Olympic final of the 400m hurdles: 54.03 seconds.

During 1989 I continued my transfer to the 400m hurdles. The number of occasions in which I ran in the 100m hurdles were from now on strictly rationed, because I could feel myself getting better and better at the longer race. For most big championships after 1989 I usually ran only two events: the 400m hurdles and the 4 × 400m relay.

I had no big wins or new records in this year, but I did end the season ranked number 3 in the world for the 400m hurdles. I also treated the world (or, at least, a big crowd in a stadium in Italy) to the inglorious sight of myself falling over in a race. I simply got my strides wrong between hurdles seven and eight, and ran too close to the eighth to be able to jump it correctly. I duly banged into it, and went sprawling.

At the beginning of 1990 I flew to Auckland for the Commonwealth Games. Like everyone else I knew that this was likely to play havoc with my training schedule, and indeed I was to find, in the latter part of the season, that I paid the price. I felt that I had lost focus, and several sports commentators observed that I seemed to lose momentum after the Commonwealth Games.

Truly, though, these Games were for me the highlight of the year. By this time I saw my principal event as the 400m hurdles, and of the three events in which I took part this came first. My main rival here was Debbie Flintoff-King, who had so outstandingly taken the Olympic gold medal in Seoul. She knew that I badly wanted to beat her; I knew that she equally badly wanted me not to. Again, it was a good race, and I took the gold with the relatively slow time of 55.38 seconds. Debbie came second, and was generous in her congratulations afterwards.

Running the 100m hurdles presented me with something of a novelty: this was the first time in my career that I was a defending champion in a major championship. My 100m hurdles title was coveted by several runners, and because I had not been running this race very often I was considered vulnerable.

In the event we had a good race, but the British hurdler Kay Morley-Brown, who ran a personal best of 12.91 seconds, beat me for first place. I came in second, at 13.12 seconds.

Towards the end of the Games the 4 × 400m relay was won by the British team, in which I ran the last leg.

I felt that two gold medals and a silver made up a good haul.

Later in the year I did poorly in the European Championships in Split, coming sixth, but I helped win a bronze in the 4 × 400m relay. In the European Cup I came second in the 400m hurdles, behind Margarita Ponomaryova.

I spent 1991 moving purposefully towards the World Championships, which were to take place in Tokyo in August. Everything clicked into place, and there were no interruptions to training. At the beginning of the season I was appointed British Team Captain, a tremendous honour.

The only upheaval in life was voluntary, and we got it out of the way before the season was in full swing. In May we finally managed to sell our flat in Brighton (the property boom had gone into sharp reversal, and we had been trying to sell for ages), and moved out to a cottage in Patcham, on the northern edge of Brighton. With ourselves and our cat safely installed, I set off on my usual summer of travelling.

I had a good season. Amongst many other 400m hurdles races were the Europa Cup and the Grand Prix, in both of which I came second. I also broke the British record in two consecutive races, the first in Monaco and the second in Zürich. At the European Cup in Frankfurt, in June, our relay team won the bronze in the 4 × 400m, setting a new British record of 3 minutes 22.01 seconds.

But the main event of the year was undoubtedly the World Championships in Tokyo. I saw this as a sort of rehearsal for the Olympics the following year, and my first real chance to show what I could do in the 400m hurdles when I would be against all the world's top hurdlers.

I was in peak condition by the time I got to Japan. I felt I ran well in the heats. Jon agreed with me on the phone from home, as he was watching everything I did on TV. He said anything he could think of to try and spur me on! Both Jon and Bruce were being most encouraging, and at last I felt I was in with a chance of winning a major championship.

I try not to let anyone other than Jon and Bruce influence me, but before the race several commentators saw me as a real contender for the gold medal. My main rival was Sandra Farmer-Patrick, the American, but she had been suffering from lower back compression, and only a week before the championships could not raise her leg to the height of a hurdle. Intensive therapy in Tokyo allowed her to compete, but she was not on her best form. The other one I had to measure up to was Tatyana Ledovskaya, from Belarus, the reigning European Champion. She is one of sport's permanent outsiders; you hardly ever see her during the year, so you have no way of knowing what kind of form she is in, then she turns up at the big matches. She has a very strict coach, and when you see her at the warm-up track he's always shouting at her. You can't pretend not to notice! On the day of the World final I saw her running six times around the track, flat out. Both her legs were taped up, as if she was injured. Bruce saw me looking at her, and he caught my eye. I grinned at him: I was just interested. I wasn't going to let her psych me out!

She had only just scraped through her semifinal, which is why I was better placed than she was: I had Lane 5 and she was in Lane 6. Even so, I was wary of her. She is famous for her extrovert style of running. She tears away from the starting line, and sometimes gains a lead of twenty metres on everyone else. It's very intimidating to follow someone like that! But she doesn't have a strong finish, and in the 400m hurdles the finish is all-important.

One of the reasons people felt I had a chance was that I was better at finishing.

The race itself mostly followed the expected pattern. From the pistol, Ledovskaya accelerated away like an electric hare. I set off after her, and by steady running started to make up ground. At the eighth hurdle (always the significant one) I felt I had her, and by hurdle nine I was almost abreast of her. If I kept up this progress I knew I could win.

Unfortunately, as I came up to hurdle ten I realized I was too close to it, and I suddenly lost confidence. I had to stutter, alter my strides, and in doing so lost the race. By the time I was clear of the hurdle Ledovskaya was well ahead of me, and although I managed to make up a little of the lost time in the dash to the line, she beat me to it.

This race was also notable for a minor incident that at the time I saw as fairly irrelevant, but which in the following weeks hung around to irritate me. As we went over the last hurdle, Sandra Farmer-Patrick and I were side by side. I was stuttering, but so too was Sandra, and as she came down to the ground she stumbled slightly and brushed against me. I felt her hand touch my arm, and that was all. As far as I was concerned it had no effect on the outcome of the race, and I gave it no more thought. Think how galled I was, a little later, when I heard Sandra's version of the same event: that I had bumped into *her*, and slowed her down! I kept hearing this repeated over the weeks that followed.

Well, I got the silver medal! My time of 53.16 seconds was another British and Commonwealth record! After the initial disappointment at not coming first, I was soon smiling unstoppably.

The Olympic medal was still what I wanted most, but those Games were to come the following year. I had no idea then, but 1992 was destined to be a momentous year, and not entirely for the reasons I expected.

Chapter 9

The Burdens of Being an Athlete

As far as money is concerned, British athletics is presently at a sort of halfway house. As I have explained, the amateur clubs are the roots of the sport in this country, and if some of them cannot be run for love then maybe they should not be run at all. At the other end of the sport, however, it is possible for athletes at the very top to earn large sums of money.

This is one of those questions that can be argued for a long time, but the main argument in favour of more money coming into the sport is that it would buy certain commodities that are at present in short supply.

It could buy time for athletes, for instance. Like almost everyone else, I had to snatch whatever time I could out of my everyday life to keep training, to keep fit, to keep competing. Every year dozens, perhaps hundreds, of young athletes may fall by the wayside because of these difficulties. If it was possible in some way for money to be used to create a financial safety-net for young athletes, then maybe we would not lose so many up and coming stars.

Facilities are another area where Britain does not lead the world. How many indoor tracks are there in *your* nearest town, for instance? How many clubs have their own grounds, their own tracks? How many have properly equipped gymnasiums? How many even have a proper clubhouse?

This is made a real issue for me when I go to the USA for warm-weather training. For instance, when I go to Tallahassee, the state capital of Florida, I train at the State University track. This is a fine track with every facility an athlete needs, and it was all paid for by local businesses. Not even the National Sports Centre in Britain has the equipment they have at this relatively small, relatively obscure American university. Quite apart from the excellence of the facilities for the athletes, it gives a large number of local people a real stake in the university's sports activities. When the team wins, *they* feel as if they're winning. When I was in Tallahassee at the beginning of 1994, the Seminoles, the university football team, had won their league championship. It seemed that just about everyone in town was wearing Seminole sweatshirts that week, and they all turned out for a huge parade through the centre of town. In Britain, we stick up loyally for our local football team, or our athletes, but we don't provide *practical* support. I believe that if we did, more ordinary people would feel much more committed, much more involved. I've always found that people I've had contact with through sponsorship are now amongst my most avid fans. Because they are putting something practical into my running they are getting much more out of it.

The traditional argument against too much money flooding into the sport is that it would distort the reasons for trying to win. In short, it would create more motive for cheating.

Of course, athletes do earn money from competing now, but until quite recently their amateur status was preserved by the maintenance of trust funds. All earnings went into these, to be set aside for the future. Athletes did have access to the money, but they had to go to the British Athletics Federation (BAF) any time they wanted some of it.

This system is now being discontinued, so trust funds may optionally be administered by the athlete's own appointed agent (mine is administered by my accountants). The BAF still has access to them, as they can inspect the books at any time to make sure the money is being used correctly, but in general the money is more under the control of the individual who has earned it.

Some people deplore the whole idea of money going into sport, claiming that amateur status should be maintained at all costs. But if this is so, why should athletics be any different from football, for example, or tennis? It is difficult to see how football could be played at the national or international level without all the money that goes into it.

The same people who stoutly defend our amateur status are the first to watch us when we run on television. Do they think that the television coverage is free? Should not some of the money that comes into the sport from TV coverage reach the people who are actually competing?

Consider this. When I run for my country I don't get paid. This includes nearly all of the most famous and popular championships: the World, Commonwealth, European, Olympics, the Europa Cup . . . all these are meetings for which I get no payment. Perhaps this is how it should be. But nonetheless money is being paid to the organizers! As the American athletes are now pointing out, the IAAF (International Amateur Athletics Federation) is making millions from selling TV rights. Why should the organizers be the only ones to get the money, they argue. So they have been campaigning to get prize money paid to the competitors, and already some progress has been made. For example, at the Stuttgart World Championships in 1993 all the winners were given a car.

One fact of which all athletes are painfully aware is how short their careers are. It takes years to get to the top; in my case I was twenty-two before I went to my first Olympics and twenty-six before I won my first gold. Other athletes take even longer – Linford Christie, whose first Olympic appearance was in the same year as mine, in 1988, was six years older. Athletics is a young person's sport; you cannot continue at your best very far into your thirties.

All this has a bearing on one's attitude to money. The period when you are paid is never more than about four or five years, and this represents the main part of the income you are likely to receive in your life!

But the argument about cheating is a compelling one.

After a sensational winning run at the Seoul Olympics in 1988, the Canadian sprinter Ben Johnson won the 100m gold medal with a world record time of 9.79 seconds. Following a drug test (all Olympic winners are routinely tested), Johnson was found to have been using a prohibited substance. He was stripped of his medal and record, and returned to Canada in disgrace.

A case less well known to the public at large is the one of the American middle-distance runner Butch Reynolds, holder of the world record for the 400 metres. After a meeting in Monaco he tested positive for a drug called Nandrolene, an anabolic steroid. Although he protested his innocence he was suspended by the IAAF. He sued them in the USA for damages and loss of earnings, and the court found in his favour, awarding him some $27 million! (This case is still rumbling on, as the IAAF has not accepted the jurisdiction of the court.)

In 1993 the death occurred at the age of thirty-six of

a hammer thrower called Detlef Gerstenberg. He died of hepatitis and pancreatic cancer, brought on, so it is claimed by his family, by the steroids and testosterone administered to him under East Germany's drugs programme.

Control and elimination of doping is therefore a matter of urgent concern to all athletes and, indeed, sports administrators. The trouble is that there are many rules and regulations, and many governing bodies, all with their own sets of rules. Most athletes strongly support the idea of random testing for drugs, but they want to be sure that it really is random, that it is carried out in the same way in every country, and that the same rules apply to everyone.

At the moment, because the governing bodies haven't got their act together everywhere, you never really know who is doing drugs and who isn't. You have to assume no one is, but it's no good worrying about it. Ninety-nine per cent of British athletes are clean, you can be sure of that, but because every athlete knows how sports administration can be politicized, and how vested interests can get their way, you can never be sure of athletes from other countries. This is not a good feeling, but if I was to worry about it I probably would not have been able to do what I have done.

This is one of those areas where you can surround yourself with negative thoughts to the point where they damage your performance. If I was to look at every competitor I raced against and think, 'Is *she* on drugs? And what about *her*?', I'd be so distracted I would lose every race.

The only thing you can do is get out there and do what you have to do without drugs. After I had won the Olympics in Barcelona, several people, including at least five members of the British team, came up to me and said, 'One of the best things about your win is the knowledge that we can do it without having to take something.'

The whole subject is a tricky one, for these reasons and

others. Scientifically, there's a real struggle going on between people who are trying to develop performance-improving drugs that can't be detected, and the authorities who are trying to detect them. The bad guys are always one step ahead, but it *is* getting better. New ideas for testing, and new techniques, are coming up all the time.

At the moment the tests are carried out on urine, but the authorities are just about to bring in blood testing. This can apparently test for drugs taken up to two months earlier, which will be an improvement. But look at it from the point of view of someone like me, who has to take a lot of tests after events. How many times can I give a blood sample in the few weeks of the racing season without doing myself harm?

The urine tests are difficult enough as it is! Imagine the sheer excitement of running and winning a major race, often in a summer climate. I'm high, happy, distracted . . . and dehydrated! And in a short period of time after the end of a race I have to report to the dope testing centre and fill a specimen bottle for the officials. This is something, I can say for certain, that you do not feel like doing.

In some ways I prefer the random tests, even though they have their own problems attached. For instance, the testers are supposed in theory to telephone in advance and let you know they're on the way, but quite often they just turn up at the house.

The last time it happened to me I did get a bit of warning. I came home on a Sunday evening to find a message on the answerphone. A woman's voice simply said, 'Please would you ring me back as soon as possible?' She left no name, just a number. In fact, she's not allowed to say who she is, but my mind was on other things so I didn't put two and two together. I thought it was someone wanting me to do an interview, or something like that, so I got my agency to ring up and find out what was going on. The woman said to them, 'Oh no, I can't speak to you. You've got to get Sally to ring me herself, and to make it straight away.' I still didn't realize what it was. When I rang her back, she said, 'You can probably guess what it is.' The moment she said that, the penny dropped at last! She came round the next day.

What followed was the standard procedure. The idea is that both the athlete and the testers should be protected from fraud. From the athlete's point of view you want to be sure that the sample you give is properly labelled and identified, and can't be interfered with after you've provided it. From the tester's point of view, she has to be certain that the sample you give is genuinely your own. It makes for an uncomfortable few minutes. Once the procedure of giving a sample begins we cannot leave each other's company.

It begins with the filling out of a form. This has several copies, but only the top one shows my name. I keep this one. Lower down the tester fills in certain other practical details, such as the time and date, where the test took place, and so on. When we have both signed the form the collection procedure has formally begun.

The tester will have brought with her five different sets of two bottles, one labelled A and the other B; I have to select one set. I don't suppose there's much between them, but I have to be as certain as possible that no one else has used the bottles before me, and that they have not been tampered with in some way. Having a choice helps eliminate this possibility. I then have to pick a little jug, and the really hard bit begins. Trying to pee into a pot with a complete stranger watching you is not only unpleasant and humiliating, it can also be difficult to accomplish. There is no way out of this, and there are no easy alternatives. Sometimes it's so hard to do that you have to turn on taps, or try to distract yourself by chatting inanely about the weather. In the end it does eventually happen . . .

With the little jug filled (you have to produce a minimum of 70ml, about a fifth of a pint) you open up the bottles and put most of the sample into Bottle A. The rest goes into Bottle B.

Up to this point the tester has been watching me like a hawk; now I start watching *her*. I never let her out of my sight once she's got my sample, because how would I know that she had not slipped something into it? Remember when these people turn up at my house they are complete strangers, and although they carry official identification from BAF, I still have to be very careful. If the future of your entire career hangs on this test, you can be excused for being concerned about scrupulous fairness.

Once the tops are back on the bottles, they are placed inside the box they came in. Then two security seals are used to close the tops, and these too are plugged into the box. You check that the numbers inscribed on the sides of the jars have been recorded properly on the form, and that the seals are identified properly. When you're satisfied that everything is as it should be, you allow the tester to close the box, and she then leaves.

The samples are taken to the Drug Control and Testing Centre, at King's College in London, where Bottle A is analyzed for banned substances. If that test proves negative, then that's the end of the matter. Both samples are destroyed, and a routine letter from BAF follows in a few days.

If the test proves positive, BAF contacts you and you are suspended from competition with immediate effect. You are required to produce an explanation, and you are summoned to the laboratory where Sample B will be tested in your presence. If this too proves positive, then the suspension is confirmed. Amid great publicity and personal humiliation you will be banned from sport for a considerable period of time. Although an appeal is allowed, if the forensic evidence is against you then you have little chance of having the ban reversed.

The whole subject is a minefield. Drugs come in many forms, many of them popular remedies freely available over the counter. No list of safe remedies would ever be complete, and because new medicines are constantly coming on to the market it would never be reliable. Furthermore, a remedy thought to be safe today could easily be banned tomorrow.

The problem would be easier to control if the banned substances were clearly identifiable. They are not. Fortunately, you can't wander into your local chemist and idly pick up a bottle of anabolic steroids to help your athletic performance. The kind of drugs that cause all the trouble are usually compounds or formulations, containing a cocktail of many different substances. Some of the most dangerous drugs are 'designer' drugs; so great are the financial rewards for cheating successfully that it is quite possible for some athletes or their coaches to have specific stimulants or muscle developers expensively created for them in a laboratory. These are the hardest drugs of all to detect, of course.

At the other end of the spectrum, there is an element of innocent drug use that can get you into trouble just as easily. For instance, if you suffer from asthma and take ephedrine for it, you will be using a banned stimulant that will test positive and get you suspended.

What about that brand-name cough mixture, found in every chemist shop and supermarket in the country? Can you be sure, completely sure that it contains nothing harmful? Suffering from the runs while waiting to compete in a foreign country? Don't take a diarrhoea remedy containing codeine or morphine, because either of those will end your career!

Even natural products might contain traces of banned substances: Linford Christie came perilously close to a ban at the Seoul Olympics after innocently drinking some ginseng tea.

Broadly speaking, the drugs you have to be wary of are stimulants, narcotic analgesics, anabolic steroids, beta blockers, diuretics, growth hormones, local anaesthetics and corticosteroids, any painkillers that contain codeine or caffeine, and hayfever treatments that contain ephedrine.

In practice there is only one safe rule, and that's to take no drugs at all. It just isn't worth the risk. These days if I catch something I let it take its natural course, suffer the effects and hope for the best.

I've got to the point now where I try not to bother with medicines. By the time I've gone through the whole list I'm too discouraged to try! I don't even use throat pastilles any more. If I get a cold I just let it happen. I used to take Night Nurse when I was training, because it dried me out and I could carry on with my training. Now I won't touch it, so if I've got a cold I'm out there in the wind and rain, running and feeling groggy! Vitamin C and zinc are safe preventatives against colds, although before I take them I always ring up my doctor, or ask the athletics doctor. It's not essential, but I do it for peace of mind. In general, if I'm ill I reduce my level of training until I feel a bit better.

The situation remains a jungle, and it is one full of pitfalls. Even BAF admits that many commonly used medicines, including those prescribed by doctors, contain banned substances. They advise checking everything with your doctor, but even they can't check every prescription if there's no reliable list of banned substances.

Even a cup of coffee endangers you. Caffeine is a banned

drug, and if you drink too much coffee you could be done for that. I'm fortunate in that I've never drunk much coffee in the last few years. I drink water and herbal tea instead.

On the other hand, some of the banned substances can only be taken purposely. Steroids are an example of this. You never swallow a few steroids by accident. Taking steroids requires a planned drugs régime coupled with intensive physical training over a long period of time.

But you always have to remember that different countries have different rules, and so do different organizations! (For example, the IAAF, which administers the Grand Prix competitions, has its own list of banned and permitted substances, many of which differ from BAF's.)

There is another element that adds to the general difficulties. You have to remember the amount of physical training we do means that we use up our bodily resources much more quickly than non-athletes. Our bodies need replenishment. Food alone is not enough to replace the vitamins and minerals we use up. If you fail to take extra vitamins, you will inevitably suffer for it. At the lowest level, you will have colds the whole time, and you won't be able to perform at your best in summer. Vitamins help you to keep your strength up.

The importance of random drug testing was brought home to me a couple of years ago when I experienced a misunderstanding whilst I was warm-weather training in Arizona.

The rule is that when you are away from home for more than five days you have to inform the British Athletics Federation, where you are going, the address of where you will be staying, and the exact dates of your stay. We did this in the usual way with a fax and letter before leaving England. However, once we arrived we found that the accommodation we had booked was unsuitable so we moved to an apartment block about a mile away. Bruce and his wife Julie remained at the original address as it was suitable for their requirements.

It wasn't until we arrived back in England that BAF informed us that the tester had visited us and was unable to make contact, even though Bruce, my coach, was still at the original address. Obviously, we had to explain to BAF exactly what had happened and supply them with details of our movements, including the training areas we used and the restaurants we frequented.

This experience highlighted to me how thorough the random testing has to be to work efficiently, and it is comforting to know that everything is being done to discourage those who may be tempted to cheat.

Chapter 10

Focusing on a Race

One of the key techniques Bruce has taught me is that at the highest levels of sport the difference between the performance of individual athletes is measurable only in tenths or hundredths of a second. Any technique that will tighten those fractions has to be used.

Bruce has always argued that mental energy must be directed into the race just as much as physical energy. However, although you can train your body physically by sheer persistence, it's much harder to train your mind. In effect, to focus the concentration on what you're doing.

Everyone suffers from distraction, in ways I need not list here. But in athletics there is a great deal to contend with: the electric atmosphere of a big stadium filled to capacity can both help and hinder, a day of blustery wind can set up worries about how your performance might be affected, and as for the other competitors . . .

Some athletes set out deliberately to psych their competitors: they turn up in flashy kit, or they talk loudly to their coach about the race, or they do some unusual or attention-getting exercise in the warm-up. Others seem to do it naturally. I'm pretty sure Tatyana Ledovskaya didn't wrap her legs in tape just to make the other girls wonder what she was up to, and I'm certain that Yordanka Donkova didn't have her fingertips amputated just to distract me in the World Championships . . . but the effect was the same.

Negative thoughts lead to a negative performance; the connection is as straightforward as that. The solution is to focus on the race. This means firstly to keep the concentration as unbroken as possible, and secondly to try to change any negative thoughts into positive ones.

I am often seen before a race lying on my back in a bit of shade, my eyes closed. I'm not catching forty winks. I'm thinking about the race, preparing mentally for it. In the last few moments before the race begins you will usually see me looking straight ahead down the track. To some people it might seem like an aggressive stare, but in reality I'm simply visualizing what I have to do.

Bruce sometimes says he sees part of his job as turning negatives into positives. He knows me so well now that he can always sense what I might be thinking, or might be about to think. Before a big race he talks me through it, putting the emphasis on positive things: I've trained enough to be able to win, my form is better than that of so-and-so competitors, and so on.

Because of the importance of the Barcelona Olympics my preparations for it began almost as soon as the previous season ended. My attitude to Barcelona was completely different from my approach to Seoul. Then, it was enough for me to compete and do well. My attitude had changed even from the previous year. In 1991 it was enough for me to win a World Championship medal but this time, I would be going to Barcelona intending to win.

My physical training continued along the same sort of lines as always. After all, the time I'd run in the 400m hurdles in Tokyo was still a phenomenal one for me: 53.16

seconds, which was only just over a fifth of a second slower than the existing world record. (Marina Styepanova, of the Soviet Union, had held the world record of 52.94 seconds since 1986.) So we realized that my level of training was right, and that my strength and speed were at a level where I was physically able to win.

(Every year, Bruce slightly increases my level of training, but only by tiny percentage points. For example, we might cut a recovery period down by fifteen seconds, or add an extra rep on the end of each session. Another way would be for me to work through a series of track sessions which total about 1,800 metres, and then he will reorganize them later in the season so that they add up to 1,900 metres.)

Simply because I had always had the power to focus on a race, I had never felt the need to sharpen my mental training. But after the Tokyo World Championships, Jon and I sat down one evening and talked through the race, almost step by step. He felt I should have won it, and kept saying so. I told him that the problem was the last hurdle: because I had suddenly lost my confidence I'd stuttered, whereas what I should have done is gone for it, taken that last hurdle anyway. David Hemery, the former athlete, had once talked to me about focusing on races, and how to think them through step by step.

At the end of this conversation, Jon had said, 'If you're thinking like that now we've got to make sure you're not by the time you get to Barcelona. Otherwise the same thing might happen again. It isn't a physical thing, because we both know you had trained hard enough in 1991.'

Afterwards, I sat down and thought about it in more practical detail. For instance, I worked out the actual times of going across hurdles. I thought, 'If I can go through the fifth hurdle in such-and-such a time, then I only have to come in at . . .' All of a sudden it felt like something I could do; the race became a series of achievable goals.

I began to see the whole race in my imagination. David had said this, 'Go through it in your mind, from the sound of the gun going off to actually crossing the line.' It seemed obvious when he said it like that, but as I learnt to imagine I began to see it in a new way.

I would imagine myself on the blocks, waiting for the gun. When the bang came I would monitor myself running to the first hurdle, and going over that first hurdle and doing it perfectly! After that hurdle, I would imagine my usual stride pattern of fifteens. I would count the fifteen, and take the second hurdle . . . and continue on all the way around. When I reached the hard bit, when I change down at the seventh so that I hurdle with the other leg, I would imagine I was doing a sixteen stride. Take the hurdle, then run sixteens all the way to the tenth.

Because the most important thing that went wrong in 1991 was between hurdles nine and ten, I would focus on that part of the race, imagining myself running hard between nine and ten, really going for the hurdle. With that behind me I would run as fast as I could to the line.

The second approach I began was to visualize different problematical situations that might arise in reality, and would have to be dealt with. I found that if I could anticipate them, they did not seem so bad.

Suppose I were to be allocated Lane 1, for example. This would normally be a minor disaster. Now I would rehearse it in my mind, trying to develop a strategy for coping with the problem. Another disaster scenario would be if I happened to draw Lane 8. Or, another, if I drew Lane 6 and Sandra drew Lane 5, and she overtook me down the back straight and was still ahead of me at the eighth hurdle. So I would focus on being able to come past her, keeping relaxed.

I went through every situation that could possibly arise, then imagined the best way of dealing with it.

Ever since the time I was preparing for the Barcelona Olympics I have been focusing on the whole business. I start with the warm-up, and what that will feel like. Then I rehearse going through the reporting and check-in. I try to imagine the stadium itself, what it will smell and sound like, what I will see, what it might feel like to be there.

If I think anything might be about to happen, no matter how small or large, I focus on it in advance, and by anticipating it I learn to deal with it.

All this visualization did not come to me in a flash. I had to work at it, and learn how to use it. In other words, it's not a magical solution that can be applied by anyone to anything. I believe you have to be equipped with the will to run these races, to be motivated to win, and to be able to back all this up with physical ability. With these already established, then the ability to visualize will give you that extra something.

Just how difficult it is can be illustrated by one of the first times I tried to focus on a whole race from beginning to end. As the end of the imaginary race approached I found I had trouble keeping the focus sharp, and seeing myself actually crossing the line first. I knew that if I let that happen then when it came to the real race I wouldn't cross the line first!

I forced myself to stop before I reached the line . . . a kind of emergency halt! I made myself 'rewind the film', and go all the way back to the start of the race. I did the race all over again, this time making sure that I won. I found it extremely difficult to do this.

One final thing I have learned from pre-visualization, Bruce has always taught me to conserve energy, so that as soon as I've done my warm-up, that's it: no more activity.

I have found focusing on a race soothing and reassuring, so that I usually go into a real race in a calm frame of mind. Quite often I have been there at the start of a race with the other girls and they're leaping up and down, burning up energy, still trying to do their warm-ups while they're waiting. I keep still. I know my body is ready, and I'm keeping the energy in it all bundled up, ready to be released when I need it most.

1992 was not my best year for form. I usually start a season by running a 400 metres flat for Essex Ladies, and after that go on the following week to a 200 metres in the UK Championships. I then make my first 400 metres hurdles my third or fourth race into the season. This is usually a smallish race: maybe one of the Grand Prix meetings, but one where the Americans haven't yet bothered to turn out. Early in the season of an Olympic year they will be doing their trials, so they would not field many top athletes at such a meet.

I did moderately well as the Olympics approached, but I did not, to give some measure of my form, break the British record at all in 1992. My best times in the pre-Olympic period were in the region of 54.20 seconds or 54.40 seconds. Three weeks before Barcelona most of the Olympic team went up to Gateshead for a meeting, but because of an injury to my thigh I was not able to take part. In addition, Sandra Farmer-Patrick had beaten me a couple of times in recent weeks.

All this makes up a classic example of how my focusing helps me deal with these kinds of situation.

Looking at it one way, I could say, 'I've been injured, I haven't been able to improve on my own British record, I haven't run well all season, and on top of all that my greatest rival keeps beating me!'

Put like that it mounts up into recipe for failure, a compendium of negative thoughts. It would amount to me psyching myself out, and would lead, inevitably, to defeat.

However, when I focused on all this I could convert it into a positive version that not only made me feel much more optimistic, it gave me the motive to win.

I said, in effect, 'the injury is slight, and my physiotherapist can deal with it. The record is still mine, and no one else's. I know how fast I am, I know how strong I am. I have never been better prepared than this. The season so far has been a build-up to the most important race, and I have not yet peaked. And Sandra is going into the Olympics as the favourite in our event; no one expects me to be able to beat her, and so all the pressure will be on her, not on me.'

Chapter 11

Olympic Gold

Before a major championship I normally spend two weeks exclusively devoted to training. In 1992, most British athletes went to Monte Carlo for their preparations, but we went to Portsmouth!

I had two excellent weeks, concentrating on precise timing and speed. For some reason I found myself absolutely flying along, with record touchdown times, and this gave me a tremendous amount of confidence. As I have said, 1992 had not to this point been a good year for me: my times were slow, and Sandra had beaten me a couple of times. But the two weeks in Portsmouth helped put all that right.

I flew into Barcelona five days before the first of my heats. The British team managers tried to fly us out as a team, and allocated three flights that the team could take. For all the usual reasons I didn't want to arrive too early, so I chose the latest possible flight. I was so late leaving, in fact, that I had been able to watch the opening ceremony and some of the events on TV at home!

We were met at the airport, then taken straight to the Olympic village, where we went through all the usual accreditation, passport checks, baggage search, and so on, before being given a pass for the village.

Exploration of the village revealed that contrary to the rumours and warnings that had been going around before I left England, it was really rather splendid. We had heard it said that the Spanish were still building the place, the flats were shabby, there was no proper ventilation, and so on. It sounded like the bad old days on the Costa Brava, but none of this was true.

In common with other places I had visited, the Olympic village consisted of high blocks of flats that would obviously be sold on later. (Mind you, I gather that in practice a large number of the Barcelona ones are still unsold.) The village was vast, and occupied an area down by the harbour, about half an hour from the athletics stadium. The apartment I was allocated in the village happened to be quite near the accreditation area, and therefore close to the main entrance, but I know that some of the other Games participants had to walk miles to get out.

The British Olympic Association (who must have moved fast to secure us places that were so convenient) had their headquarters in the village. This was an impressive place, clearly carefully planned to cope with the all the paperwork of the Olympics, meetings of officials, briefings for journalists, the various needs of the athletes, communications with the outside world, and so on.

Near our apartment building was a row of places where we could take out magazines, books, groceries, and so on, all free of charge. There were even the inevitable hamburger and fast-food joints, as well as a large general restaurant, which quickly became a central meeting point for most people. Again, all these were free to athletes carrying passes. All the major sports companies had their own places, and because a lot of the athletes were directly or indirectly sponsored by such companies, this meant that their presence provided one more haven of calm amid the bustle.

In all, the village facilities were better than any I had previously experienced; miles ahead of Seoul, of course, but better even than those in Tokyo the previous year.

Ten of us were crammed into our apartment, with two to each bedroom; I was sharing with my old friend Jenny Stoute. The accommodation was basic – a kitchen, a lounge with a TV and enough chairs, two bathrooms, and sufficient storage space for all our kit so, considering the short time we were going to be there it was not at all bad. Knowing the weather would be hot I'd taken a fan out with me. Jenny and I slept with the windows open and the fan on.

On my first evening we all went to a team meeting; I was of course there in my capacity as captain of the women's team, but none of the officials gave me any advance hint or warning of what was to come.

Brusquely, shockingly, we were told that one of our team had tested positive for drugs, that he had been summoned from his room late the preceding evening, and was already back in England. His name was Jason Livingstone, a 100 metres runner who had recently won a European Indoors competition. Apparently he had been caught in June, but they had decided to wait until the Olympics before telling us (or him).

There we were, all hyped up, excited and ready to go, and they suddenly hit us with this. The British Sports Council had made a decision to hold on to his drugs sample until this moment, clearly thinking it would have more impact on us if they told us while we were all together at the Olympics. I was inevitably reminded of my own experience after my warm-weather training in Arizona earlier in the year.

The effect, on me at least, was quite the opposite of what they appeared to intend. I imagine they thought it would shock us into some kind of outraged action, spurring us to greater efforts in the Games. Instead, everyone looked stunned, demoralized and depressed. We had gone to the meeting in an expectant frame of mind, all looking forward to taking part, and we left feeling miserable, worried and anxious.

As soon as I could I found out where the buses left from (this turned out to be just outside the row of shops, so these too were convenient for us), and made my usual visit to the warm-up area, and so on, to do a quiet recce. The good news was that the warm-up area was close to the main stadium, and there was a lot of grass on which I could do my strides, but the bad news was that the warm-up area did not appear to have much shade. I remember being impressed by the high level of security: there were police and armed guards everywhere you looked.

Another aspect of Barcelona that I liked was that there seemed to be training facilities everywhere. There was a track actually within the village compound itself, and another not far down the road towards town. Because the one in the village was understandably crowded most of the time, I chose to use the other. The first time I trained there Daley Thompson came over to watch me, and a little later Brendan Foster from British TV came along. Brendan asked me how I thought the 400m hurdles would go, but I was as cagey as I could be without seeming to be rude.

Later, they were all watching while I trained, and of course I chose that moment to stutter as I went over one of the hurdles! I probably didn't look like much of a potential gold medallist, and just then I certainly didn't feel like one.

The next day I went down to the main stadium and observed my ritual of watching Linford Christie run his 100m hurdles, but apart from this I treated it as a day of total rest. All my main training had been finished in Portsmouth, so now it was simply a case of staying in trim.

Once I was back in the village after watching Linford I could feel the dreaded lethargy creeping up on me again. I went to the restaurant and sat there for two or more hours, just chatting with anyone who came by, but all the time trying simultaneously to fight off the mood of nervous depression and to conserve physical energy. I was waiting all day to know the positions for the heats, but as bedtime approached the information had still not been released. Remember that for me the prospect of the heats is more terrifying than the final itself. To be beaten into second or third place in a final is one kind of defeat, but the failure to qualify even for a run in a final is much worse. I have never grown used to this, in all the years I have been competing. I decided to stop worrying about it until the morning.

Luck was with me: I turned out to be not only in a good heat (the last one), but also in a good position: Lane 4. I went out to the stadium, warmed up, then out to the track. Sandra Farmer-Patrick was already through to the semifinal, as were Tatyana Ledovskaya and Margarita Ponomaryova. In my own heat were Tonja Buford from the USA and Irmgard Trojer from Italy, both of whom I had raced against in recent weeks.

I won my heat by quite a distance and in a good time: in fact at 54.98 seconds it was the fastest time in all the heats, and very close to the fastest I had run all year. Because I was aiming to conserve energy for the semifinal the next day, I slowed down at the end once I knew I was well in the lead, and jogged in after the last hurdle.

After I had warmed down I had a Japanese massage at the Mizuno place, to get the lactic out, then went back to the village where I had a bath and tried to forget about everything until the next day.

I was in Lane 4 again for the semifinal, and again I won this by a fair distance. My time, 53.78 seconds, was once more the fastest (Sandra, who won the other heat, came in at 53.90 seconds). Suddenly, against all the precedents of form and injury, I was the favourite for the final in two days' time.

The final was not scheduled to be held until six-thirty in the evening of that second long day. All I wanted to do was to get on with it, but I had to spend the time just sitting around in the village. I filled in the hours as best I could: I had another massage over at the Mizuno place, had a meal with Bruce, and spent a lot of time with Jenny Stoute.

Jenny had been doing really well, running her personal best and getting into the semifinals of her event, the 200m flat. This was taking place on the same day as my final, but earlier in the afternoon. Jenny and I were both high as kites, and we spent a lot of time laughing, singing silly songs, and shouting at people through the windows. None of this was behaviour that becomes the British team captain, but neither would have been the alternative. We were so nervous that if we hadn't been giggling, we'd have been crying.

I woke up on the morning of the race feeling really bad, and had to force myself to get out of bed. I went down with Jenny for breakfast and ate as much as I could, knowing that by lunchtime I wouldn't feel like eating much at all. After this I spent the morning as lazily as possible, lying on my bed and reading magazines, trying to conserve energy. I found it difficult to concentrate, even on the magazines, because thoughts of the race kept creeping in.

In the end I lay on my bed and focused closely on the race, trying to get all these random thoughts packed away into a useful piece of concentrated preparation.

After lunch (my appetite was as terrible as expected, and all I could force down was a banana and a roll) I returned to the room, had a shower, washed my hair, and got my kit ready. I was so anxious to get started, to get it all over with. When it was as late as I could force myself to wait I got into my kit, then went down and caught the bus to the stadium. I saw a couple of my competitors on the bus, but we made no eye-contact.

I realized that the next time I was on that bus my life was going to be totally different, no matter what the outcome of the final. I sat staring out of the window, watching the buildings of Barcelona going by, and thinking, 'Why the hell do I do athletics? There must be an easier way! If only I could do something else!' I know that many others go through this whenever there's a big race, notably Colin Jackson and Linford Christie.

I saw Jenny sitting with Bruce on the far side of the warm-up area, keeping in the shade under a tree. I went over and joined them. Jenny had already started warming up. She was stretching, and I lay down beside her . . . and we started singing again!

Jenny's time inevitably came around, so I wished her good luck and off she went. Bruce stayed with me. Again, the other 400m hurdles competitors were all about, but no one was looking at anyone else. I stuck to the same routine I'd always used, the same warm-up exercises, the same couple of runs over the hurdles, the same lying around in the shade. At one point I realized I had left my water bottle unattended by the side of the track, which brought on a mild attack of panic. Rumours had circulated that water bottles were being spiked with something when their owners weren't watching. I grabbed it, and kept it by my side. Ridiculous, really, but it was more ridiculous to take chances.

I watched Ledovskaya doing her flat-out runs, with straps all over her legs. If I had worries about any of the other girls, she was the one who concerned me the most. In Tokyo the year before she had performed relatively badly in the semifinal, but came out in the final and beat us all.

Bruce saw me looking.

'Just relax, Sally,' he said. 'Stop watching her.'

'It's OK,' I replied.

Just at that moment Ledovskaya crashed spectacularly into one of the hurdles, and then I really did feel OK.

They led us out into the stadium in the order of the lanes in which we would be racing, with a banner in front proclaiming our event. The stadium seemed full of noise, colour and movement. It was a hot, sultry evening, perfect weather for me. I heard the British fans shouting my name and I wanted to wave back in gratitude, but keeping my concentration was a full-time effort.

I was going to be in Lane 3, the one I liked best. Sandra Farmer-Patrick was to be in Lane 4, Tatyana Ledovskaya in Lane 8. No possible alternative arrangement could have suited me better, because I could keep an eye on them all through the early stages, and they wouldn't know where I was until it was too late.

From the starting line I did one run over the hurdles before I lay down on the side of the track. I could hear people shouting for me again, which was fantastically encouraging, but I still did not look up. I waved a hand, concentrating and focusing.

The official who was starting the race blew a whistle, which was the signal for us to take off our kit and move to the starting blocks. As ever, this was the worst time of all. We were probably made to wait only another five minutes, but it felt like an hour.

I had to force myself not to jump around, because I was so tense. I sat down on the box to conserve energy, and tried to keep my mind focused on the race. I did a little bit of leg-shaking, and stared down the track in front of me, thinking through the race, telling myself there was just one chance, only one, and this was it.

The next command was, 'On your marks.'

I moved to the blocks, stretched forward and put my weight on my hands. I crouched back into the starting position, with my hands on the line.

The stadium went quiet. All those people were suddenly silent. Everyone waited.

I was thinking, '*Go off hard. Relax a bit down the back straight. Hit it hard around the bottom bend. Then come on as strong as you can!*'

'Set.'

We all braced . . . and suddenly Ledovskaya went storming off, a millisecond before the gun.

We broke and scattered as the pistol fired a second time, the tension dissipating. Everyone hates a false start!

As I walked back to the blocks I was thinking, '*If she hadn't done that it would all be over by now!*'

There was no alternative but to go back and do it all over again. I forced myself to keep concentrating, not let it distract me. All of us were in the same position, all trying to compose ourselves.

The silence descended again on the stadium, and we got away on the second start.

Looking back, in total honesty, I have to say that the race

is a blank in my mind from the moment we started until I reached the eighth hurdle. I was so completely focused that everything that happened is confused with how I had planned it to happen. Fortunately, I have seen the videos of the race!

Tatyana Ledovskaya bombed away at an incredible pace, with Sandra Farmer-Patrick in hot pursuit. In a few seconds, Sandra had taken the lead. Both girls were setting a tremendous pace. I was third, getting into rhythm. Fifteen strides to the hurdle . . . over. Another fifteen strides . . . over. The back straight is the place for strength, for building up the position from which to accelerate into the finish.

For the first two hundred metres I was behind, but I was getting into my ideal position. I was in control. I knew how the other girls raced, and I have learnt not to panic. They always do this!

At the sixth hurdle, as I came into the bend I changed down to sixteen strides, preparing for the seventh, then the eighth, the all-important eighth. I really hit hard around that bend, on the sixth, seventh and eighth hurdles. One of my strengths is that I finish well, and it was on that bend that I went into my finish.

I came off the eighth hurdle, and I was slightly ahead of Ledovskaya and Farmer-Patrick. I thought, *'You're ahead, go for it!'*

I cleared the ninth hurdle and thought, *'Right! Attack it!'* I went over the tenth and got it right. The line was ahead and I pulled away a bit more, dashing towards the finish. I couldn't see any of the others.

I was slowing down . . . and suddenly I could hear the crowd, breaking into my isolation. The sound was so loud it was almost a physical pressure. I glanced to the side, where there was a sea of Union Jacks waving crazily. Everyone seemed to be jumping up and down. Everyone was smiling, hurling their arms around. Everyone was looking at me.

I thought, *'Is that it? Is it over?'*

The board showed my time: 53.23 seconds.

I had visualized crossing the line so often, and tried to imagine what it would feel like, but it hadn't felt like this! I had got it wrong. It was totally different!

For a moment I thought I was still visualizing, still focusing, still imagining . . . *'Is it real? I haven't actually done it. Have I?'*

Someone is going to press the button, rewind it, and I'll have to do it all over again, I thought.

Then Jenny Stoute ran from the tunnel and threw her arms around me. At that moment I knew I had won, I had really won.

Chapter 12

Barcelona 1992 – Jon's Story

While I was out there in Barcelona doing all the work, where was my boyfriend?

Let Jon take over for a while, and tell his own story:

Over the years I had fallen into the habit of not going abroad with Sally to overseas meetings. It really began when she went off to Seoul and I stayed at home to fix up the flat we were going to move into as soon as she was home. In the years that followed, it seemed to work better if she went on her own. I found I could participate just as well from home, and it more or less developed as a conscious role.

I was her hold on familiar reality: she would ring me up and we'd chat about domestic things, how the cats were, and stuff like that. At the same time, because I was usually able to watch her on TV, I could feed back to her little bits of information – such as what I thought of the other competitors, or how the heats had gone that she hadn't been running in, or what the TV commentators were saying about her, if I thought it might be useful or helpful to her.

When you're actually there at a big championship, taking part, you don't have a chance to see the larger picture. You're either warming up or cooling down, or you're out there doing your racing, or else you're trying to relax in the village by not thinking about sport at all.

For these sort of reasons, most competitors don't take their spouses with them. You just don't find much time for each other.

So when Barcelona came along I assumed I'd play my usual role, because it worked for both of us.

Although Sally had won the silver medal in the World Championships, and had done fantastically well by any standards, I still felt she could, and perhaps should, have won it. We didn't look on it as a disaster, but at heart I had so much wanted her to win. Because I see her all the time, and train with her, I know what she's capable of. I wanted her to win that Olympic gold more than words can describe!

So Sally went off two weeks before the Olympics to a training camp in Portsmouth, and from there straight to the Games. Consequently, I hadn't seen her for about two to three weeks, except briefly on television.

I watched her do her heat, and I thought, *'She's looking good.'*

The next day, the semifinals were at about 7.30 p.m. I was at work all day but I made sure I was home in time. I watched the race with a couple of friends called Johan and Rhys, and we had a great time cheering her on. One of them said, 'You've got to get across there for the final.' I tried to explain the arrangement Sally and I had, but their excitement was infectious. After they had gone I sat there on my own trying to deal with the exhilaration that was growing in me.

I thought, *'I don't know, I think she looks really, really good.'*

I spoke to her on the phone shortly afterwards, and she said she felt great. I tried to tell her what I was thinking, tried to convey not just the hope but the *confidence* that the gold medal was there for her if she wanted it. Sally sounded just like her old self, and I felt I wasn't getting across to her the special sense of encouragement I wanted to pass on.

Meanwhile, the local papers and TV station were on to me, saying, 'Can we come round and watch you watching the race?' I was thinking, *'I don't need that sort of thing at all!'* So the next day, which was Sally's rest day in Barcelona, I got up as usual and went to work in London.

Everyone in the office was saying how good Sally looked. I repeated to them what Sally had said to me over the phone the night before.

Kate, the girl who sat next to me at work, said, 'What are you doing here? You ought to be out there with her.'

'Someone else said that to me last night,' I replied.

'Then what are you waiting for?' Kate said.

The weird thing was that Sally phoned about ten minutes after that. After we'd chatted for a bit, I said as casually as I could, 'If I got a flight and came to watch the final, would you mind?'

She said she wouldn't mind at all.

I said, 'That's good, because I've just booked myself one!'

She said she could get me a ticket into the stadium, and I could pick it up from the Mizuno headquarters. She also told me how to get in touch with her at the Games. The way the system worked is that there were computers all over the Olympics, and Sally had a code she could key into. I could ring a certain number and leave a message on the computer for her.

The next thing I did was to phone my mother.

I said, 'I'm going to the Olympics, and the plane takes

off at 3.00 p.m. Can you pack me some clothes and meet me at the airport?'

I'd left myself almost no time. I put the phone down, dashed off to Gatwick, rendezvoused with my mum and caught the plane with a few minutes to spare. The flight didn't take much over an hour, and the next thing I knew I was standing in Barcelona Airport and thinking. *'Now what do I do? What's best?'* In the rush to leave the office I hadn't had a chance to plan anything at all.

I knew that Sally's parents were at the Games already, and they had told me that the company running sports tours was operating out of a hotel at the main railway station. I thought it would make sense to go there first. I located a train at the airport, and travelled into the city centre. I found the travel company's hotel straight away, and told them I wanted to stay in the same hotel as Mr and Mrs Gunnell. At this point I discovered one of the major frustrations that visitors to the Barcelona Olympics were being subjected to. Most people had been allocated hotels in outlying areas, and there was a system of trains and buses to take them in and out of town. Sally's parents were in a hotel that was two hours by train from Barcelona, and three hours by coach if the trains weren't running (which they often weren't, I was told).

It was already about 8.30 p.m., and getting to that faraway hotel just seemed impossible. I thought I'd try my luck on my own and see if the hotels in the centre of Barcelona had any vacancies. So I set off, not quite knowing where I was going or what I was looking for. Most of the hotels were full, because of the Games. My bag was getting heavier and heavier, and my spirits were low. I finally turned a street corner and plodded down a really rather narrow and dodgy road. Sally had warned me to be careful in the station area, where apparently one of the coaches had been mugged. There I was, feeling and looking so obviously like a tourist.

I decided that if I couldn't find anywhere in the next few minutes I would sleep at the station. Then I saw a smart hotel, tucked away down a narrow road.

I went to reception and asked for a room. The man said, 'Olympic race?' I didn't know what he meant; perhaps he had said, 'Olympic rates?' I asked him if this meant he had a room. He said it did, so I immediately agreed to take it for the next two nights, and gave him my credit card. He ran it off and I went up to the room. It was a tiny place with a marble floor and a single bed. It had no toilet, and no bath or shower, although there was a washbasin. I sat on the edge of the bed and looked at the receipt, trying to work out how much the room was costing me. The answer was £150 a night. I was thunderstruck! I went down to the lobby, found a telephone, and rang home. I told my dad what I'd done.

I said, 'I think I'm in trouble. If things don't work out, can I borrow some money when I get home?'

He told me to forget about it, that I'd done the right thing.

I then rang the computer number and left a message for Sally that I was at this hotel. She rang me back almost straight away and we talked as if I were still in England. We agreed not to meet. I said, 'Let's pretend I'm in England, and nothing else has changed.' We were both so used to the idea of being separated on these big occasions.

In the morning I went along to the Mizuno place and picked up my ticket. Sally's brother Paul was coming in that day, and he had done the same sort of thing as me, flying in at the last minute with nowhere to stay. He turned up at my hotel by about 1.00 p.m. Sally phoned an hour later.

I said to her, 'Best of luck. You've nothing to worry about. It's all there, you've done all the work. You've just got to really want it and it's yours.'

That's so easy to say, of course, but to go and do it is a hundred times harder!

We made tentative arrangements to meet up after the race, but we knew it was likely to be difficult.

Finally, Paul and I set out for the stadium. We took our seats, which were right by the start of the 100 metres and quite low down. We watched about an hour and a half of the athletics before Sally's race was due.

I couldn't stop thinking about Sally's final, and all the preparation she had gone through for it. Her plans were built around the eighth hurdle. We both knew that if she could get to that and be at least level with anyone else in the race, then she could win. I knew this was at the core of her strategy as we always talked about it when we were on the phone to each other.

Our seats were not in a good position from which to watch, though. Where the eighth hurdle would be placed was across from us, and the finishing line was way down to our right.

Just before Sally was due to appear, I said to Paul, 'I don't think we're in the right place here. We should be further down the straight.'

I was pretty sure the finish was going to be a close one. Every Olympic final is tightly contested, and however well Sally ran she would not be leading by ten or fifteen metres. If it was going to be a close finish I wanted to see every moment of it.

We went up to the top tier, just a few metres before the finish line. We had already discovered the officials were really strict about seating, and when we got there we found a young lady who was looking after that particular block of seats. She signalled that we couldn't watch from there.

I said, 'Please, please, *please* . . . let me watch just this one race. I'll go after that. My girlfriend is in it and I really want to watch her finish. This is her brother. We promise we'll move afterwards.' She agreed we could stay for just one race, so we crunched ourselves down, making sure that the people behind us could still see.

By this time Sally and the others were all at their starting blocks, and I watched the familiar young figure as she stared along the track.

The gun went, and they did their false start, and we waited while they lined up again. When the gun fired a second time, off she went! She looked great.

It's a funny thing, but as soon as she reached the second hurdle I could tell she was going to win. I said to Paul, 'She's got it.'

I hardly remember the rest. Round she went, and she came out of the last three hurdles like an express train. As she crossed the line we went mad! Paul and I were leaping about all over the place. I kissed the girl who had let us sit there, and then we ran all the way down to the seats where we should have been sitting. My left arm was throbbing; Paul had been thumping it all the way from the last bend!

We were still shouting and cheering along with everyone else as Sally, draped in the Union Jack, did her lap of honour. Now we were back in our original seats we were closer to the track, so we cut down to the retaining fence. As Sally came towards us Paul shouted her name, and by some miracle she heard him! She trotted over to us, and by forcing my arms through the fence I could just get them around her shoulders.

She went off, and that was it. I knew there would be no way of getting to her after a race like that. I watched her cantering off into the distance, surrounded by cameramen, other athletes, reporters and officials, until all I could see of her was a glimpse of the flag.

Then she was gone.

We went back to our seats, sat down again and watched the events that followed. Something odd crept over us. For about an hour and a half we both sat completely motionless. It was as if we had gone into shock. Finally, when Sally came out for the medal ceremony we snapped out of it. It was like coming out of a dream.

When the ceremony was over I said to Paul, 'I think it's about time we had a drink.'

We headed out of the stadium and found the nearest drinks tent, where we bought a beer each. From there we walked back to my hotel. The way down was a precipitous path, and the Spanish, very cleverly, had put beer tents at strategic points alongside. The further we went the more we felt like celebrating, so we were well oiled by the time we got to the bottom. About halfway down we happened to run into Sally's mum and dad, and as can be easily imagined we were all a little tired and emotional by then. I think we must have stopped at about half a dozen of the beer tents.

In the city centre, Paul said, 'I think I'll go back to the hotel where Mum and Dad catch their bus.'

I was undecided. I wanted to stay in the celebratory mood with them, but Sally had said she would try to ring me at my hotel after the race, and I didn't want to miss her call. In the end I decided to go back to my hotel.

I was going through the entrance doors when my arm was suddenly grabbed by an extremely attractive Spanish lady. I was pretty much the worse for wear by this time, and I stared at her in a way which for me was all exhilaration but which to her must have looked completely lecherous. She said, 'The BBC want you at the studio.' So I said, 'Yeah! Why not?'

She dragged me back outside to where a car was waiting, and off we went, dashing through the Barcelona traffic. We reached one of the main Olympic buildings; it was like going into the brightly lit nerve centre of some vast business enterprise, with telephones and computers everywhere. I was shown through a door, and beyond, in a semi-darkened room, was a pool of tranquillity bathed in light.

I could see Sally sitting at a long desk, talking quietly to Des Lynam. There were only a couple of cameras and a few technical people around. It looked like a private conversation between old friends. Somebody sidled up to me and clipped a mike to my shirt.

I went to the desk and sat down beside Sally.

Chapter 13

The Olympic Aftermath – 1

I felt as if I were wrapped in an invisible blanket, or trapped inside a cocoon. I couldn't get out and nothing else could get in. Everything had happened, and now everything felt unreal. Then I thought, *'I've got to jog around! I won!'*

Everyone was waving at me but they all seemed to be so far away. I went across to the nearest mass of Union Jacks, and the people there stretched out their arms towards me, smiling and calling my name. I touched a few hands, then someone pushed out a huge flag towards me and I grabbed it. Still the feeling of being in a cocoon persisted: I could see my hand closing on the flag, could feel it in my hand, but it didn't feel as if I was holding anything at all. Everything was detached from me, outside of me. It had that eerie quality of a slow-motion film, or of being in a dream. Nothing was making sense.

I continued jogging slowly around the track, stopping every now and then to wave and grin, brandishing the flag, and all the while thinking, *'What's going on? I don't believe any of this!'*

I hadn't gone very far – just to the first bend – when I heard my Mum calling me. Amid all that noise I actually heard her voice! She and Dad were waving frantically at me. I rushed over to them, and the cocoon suddenly lifted away, I got my arms around them and hugged and held them as tightly as I could. Auntie Dorothy and Uncle Alan were there too, slapping my back, kissing me! It was for all of us the moment of our lives! This was the first major championship that my parents had ever been to, and I had won the Olympics in front of them. Dad was crying, and this started Mum and me off!

But I had to carry on round the track. All the photographers were running about trying to get pictures of me, but I didn't want to see them: I wanted to see the crowd and the British flags. There were so many British flags there! I had not realized how many fans from home had come out to the Games. It was incredible and I was just revelling in it, glorying in it. *'This is what it's for,'* I thought. *'It's all about me, and my country, and being British, and winning.'*

I was jogging round the second bend when another minor miracle occurred: I heard Paul's voice calling me! I trotted over to him, and realized Jon was there too. We had a brief hug, but there were now so many people jostling around me it was impossible to linger.

As I jogged up the home straight I saw the British crowd, the one that had come out as a group. There was a sea of waving flags! An amazing sight! I stopped and gave them a big wave. Then someone steered me to where a whole row of photographers was waiting, and I had to pose for them. All this seemed to take ages and, even while they were still snapping away, the competitors in the next race, the men's final, were coming out behind us.

I went through the tunnel from the stadium and picked up my tracksuit. The lady responsible for the drugs test came up and gave me her standard notice that I was required to provide a sample of urine. The other girls were also out there. They clustered around to congratulate me and I took this first chance I had to speak to them. I saw the British team managers, who were all over me, which was great . . . then Bruce appeared. He told me he had watched the race on a TV monitor outside the stadium, and since then had given a long interview to Brendan Foster. He was trying to be very matter-of-fact about it all, but I noticed his eyes were distinctly red!

British television crews were there, and I gave an impromptu interview right there, with everything going on around me. I was still dizzy, but I had enough presence of mind to grab the opportunity and say thanks to all the people who had helped me. A mad whirl had already begun. A couple of press guys came up to me and started asking me for my reactions. All my defences were down, and I found myself being very open. I've learnt over the years to be fairly cagey about what I say to the press, but at that moment words just tumbled from my lips. If they'd asked me for my most intimate secret, they could have had it. Nothing had really sunk in yet.

Afterwards, I put on my tracksuit ready for the medal ceremony, then went off and brushed my hair and put on lipstick. All of a sudden I felt a little isolated: at that point there was no one around – other athletes, or even people in the team management – that I knew.

I was told to go and sit in a certain room, and when I got there I found Sandra Farmer-Patrick and Janeene Vickers already waiting. They acknowledged me with big American grins, but we really had nothing to say to each other, and after a moment or two an uneasy silence fell. There were just the three of us sitting in that room, all thinking about what had just happened out there on the track. Janeene looked fairly happy, but Sandra seemed really pissed off. After a while she began talking in a loud voice, partly to Janeene, partly to the room at large . . . but never directly to me. She was going on about *her* race! It was an excruciating experience! There I was in the last place on earth I wanted to be: shut up in a room with these two for ten slow-moving minutes.

At last the officials came for us, and we were led out into the packed stadium for the ceremony. I was in front, but not at all sure what to expect or confident that I knew what to do. The crowd roared when they saw us, and once again the Union Jacks were waving on all sides.

I was thinking, *'This is really happening! I did win!'* It was beginning to sink in, and in a big way. I felt my mood starting to lift, and I let myself get carried away by the moment.

They called out our names in Spanish, French and English. I had no idea what I was expected to do, but I stepped up calmly on to the winner's rostrum, and they gave me my gold medal. Then we stood there as the Union Jack went up and the band played *God Save The Queen* . . . and again I thought, *'I've done it! I won!'* But it was still inconceivable, it still refused to fit in with whatever I thought normality might be.

Finally the music stopped, and I was free to go mad. I jumped up and down on that rostrum as if I were demented. I had a feeling of overwhelming, uncontainable joy, one I wanted to treasure for ever.

Of course, it had to end. I shook hands with the other two, who were both smiling now. We were each given a cuddly toy and a bunch of flowers, and umpteen more photographs were taken. On my way back out of the stadium I threw the flowers into the crowd, and saw a forest of arms going up as people tried to catch them.

The whirl continued; we were ushered down to the press

The day after winning Stuttgart, 1993, on my way to Jon's hotel.

I love celebrations. This was Christmas 1987 with the Bigg family.

Showing my elation, having just won.

On the way to winning
Olympic gold in the
400m hurdles, 1992.

Hugging my parents after I had won; it was a very emotional moment for us.

In action during the last leg of the *Great Britain v Germany* relay race at RAF Cosford, 1989.

Swept off my feet by Jon and the ushers at our wedding – *(from left)* Colin Jackson, John Regis, Jon, Linford Christie and Mark McKoy.

Enjoying a glass of champagne with Jon after all the action.

Married and in possession of our licence!

Reaching for the tape in the World Championship 400m hurdles race at Stuttgart, 1993.

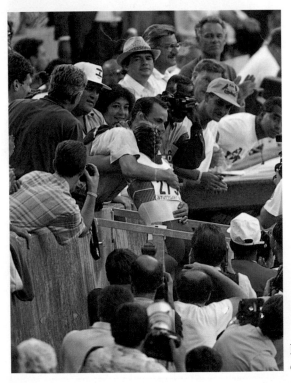

I managed to find Jon in the crowd and give him a huge hug.

The fact that I had won the gold medal and broken the world record was just beginning to sink in.

With my coach Bruce Longden, to whom I owe so much.

With Mum and Jon after I received my MBE, 1993.

room, where we had to take questions from journalists. As we went in, I was surprised to notice that there weren't all that many reporters there (although afterwards I realized that another final was going on at the same time). Most of the British journalists had turned up, of course, but not many foreigners.

We answered the questions as best we could, but at that point, still only a relatively short time after the race, I was still so stunned that to talk sensibly about the race was just about impossible. I remember that Sandra was a bit grudging: 'Sally ran a good race and I'm pleased for her', she managed. I tried to tell them about coming out of the eighth hurdle, but I knew it probably sounded like gibberish. I was finding it hard just then to describe how I tackled the race: my mind was full of memories of the happy crowd yelling at me in the humid night air and waving their flags. Sandra said that she knew if we were all together on the eighth hurdle that the finish was going to be close (but we had not all been together then and the result was not especially close).

The limit time for taking the dope test was fast approaching, so I hurried there and went through the procedure as soon as I could. As usual after a race I was as dry as a bone, and totally incapable of producing my sample. The officials are used to this: they have lots of iced beer on hand, so I helped myself to a couple of bottles and drank their contents. They went straight to my head! However, they also did the trick.

I left the dope-test centre feeling a bit woozy, and distinctly unsteady on my legs. I was just wondering what was going to happen next, when it was decided for me. A young English woman came up to me and said she was from the BBC. They wanted to interview me as soon as possible, and she said she would take me to the studio. By this time it was about nine o'clock in the evening, but it felt much later to me. I wondered briefly why British TV was still on the air; didn't they break off for the news at this time? A car rushed us to the BBC building. On my way up to the TV studio I was intercepted by a radio journalist, and did a quick interview on the spot, while the young woman waited politely. I saw Daley Thompson there, and he was grinning happily at me. Everything was starting to blur around me. I was taken through to the main presentation studio, and it was cool and spacious, with a lighted area at the end where Desmond Lynam was seated in front of two cameras. He greeted me cheerily, and I sat down and started chatting away, almost as if I was talking to my next-door neighbour. I suddenly realized why the programme was still on the air, and who they had been waiting for. My sense of unreality returned, but by now I was relaxed and happy, and a long way past caring.

Then Jon walked in and sat down beside me.

Chapter 14

The Olympic Aftermath – 2

We finished the Des Lynam interview at last, and as we were leaving the studios one of the BBC managers came up to us. He said, 'We've arranged a car and a driver for you. You can use it for anything you like.'

I was still dressed in my Olympic tracksuit, and I was carrying the gold medal, so I didn't feel there were many places I could go dressed like that.

Jon and I quickly debated what to do. Suddenly he said, 'I know where your mum and dad are. Do you want to go and see them?'

'Yeah, of course!'

I hadn't seen them since those few seconds at the edge of the track during the lap of honour, and now I had the gold medal to show them. We gave the driver the name of the hotel and he drove us straight there. We said we would probably be about ten or fifteen minutes, no longer, and he said he would wait for us.

We walked into the hotel.

That we had made a big mistake was obvious from the

moment we went through the door. The place was bursting with all the British supporters, who, like my parents, had come here to wait for their buses. I was spotted as soon as we walked in. Suddenly the atmosphere in the room, which had been full of the usual hubbub of people chatting, became electric.

Somebody shouted, *'Sally's here!'*

A great cheer went up. Everyone looked amazingly happy and enthusiastic and pleased to see me. People were shaking my hand, congratulating me, slapping me on the shoulders, stretching out to touch me. Then they started clapping, and it became a standing ovation. We were right in the middle of it! It was deafening, exhilarating . . . and terrifying! The pressure increased as more people tried to get across to us. I grabbed Jon's hand tightly, and he began trying to shoulder his way out of the crowd, smiling and being pleasant, but nevertheless having to push.

Thankfully, we suddenly saw Mum and Dad, and when people noticed we were waving to each other they at last made a space for us. We got across to them, and after a quick hug we managed to sit down somewhere with them. The crowd of people was still all around us, and the noise was tremendous. We were anxious not to seem rude, especially as someone had generously bought us a bottle of champagne which was put down on the table between us, but what we really wanted was a private talk. Finally, Jon suggested that we go out to the car park, and after a while we managed to slip away.

I was shaken up by the experience in the crowd. It was still only two or three hours since running the race, and my sense of unreality continued. In such a state, with all defences down, I was in no condition to deal with a throng like that.

It had been my first real experience of being famous, and

already I was discovering how difficult fame can sometimes be. Everyone had been happy, excited, well-meaning. They were glad to see me, and I was glad to see them . . . but there were so many of them and only one of me, and I had been, frankly, petrified.

In the relative peace of the hotel car park we had another hug, a proper chat, and of course I showed my parents my precious medal.

We had only a short time together: they had to catch their bus out to their hotel in the distant countryside.

Jon and I went back to the front of the hotel, where, rather to our surprise, considering how much longer than planned we had been, the driver was still waiting for us. We debated what to do, and where to go. However, I was still in my tracksuit, still nursing that irreplaceable medal. We wanted to go off and be alone together, but where? That crowd in the hotel had shaken me up a lot, and all of a sudden I felt that Barcelona was full of places where that might happen again. I also felt I should go back to the village. Most of the people I had worked with for all those years were there, and I wanted to see them.

After a short debate we decided to separate. Jon walked back to his hotel (where he ran into Paul again, who ended up sleeping on the cold marble floor in Jon's room), and I asked the driver to take me to the Olympic village.

It was after 11.30 p.m. when I was dropped off. Olympic athletes tend to go to bed early, so I had to walk back through the village on my own and everything was dark and still. I was struck by the contrast after all I had been doing and going through during the evening. I had been surrounded by people since the race finished, and now, abruptly, I was alone. My colleagues, perhaps the only ones who would fully understand what had happened to me, had come back to the village and, not knowing where I was, had all gone to bed.

As I went into my block of flats I saw a few people, mostly from other teams. They all congratulated me: good news travels fast in the village. I went up to our flat and crept in quietly, knowing that a couple of the girls were racing the next day. They had put up a *WELL DONE SALLY!* banner over the door, which made me happy. I opened the door of my room, and to my great surprise and pleasure Jenny was waiting up for me.

We settled down to a good old chat; she had a lot to celebrate, too, because she had run a personal best the same day. While we were talking, four of the other girls heard us and came in, and the six of us sat there for about two hours, just talking and laughing and revelling in the whole experience. It's at times like this that competing in the Olympics can make you feel that special buzz.

I didn't get much sleep that night (I put my gold medal under the pillow, for safety), and had to make an early start in the morning. This was my rest day, with the 4 × 400m relay taking place the following day, but I was having to work! An 8.00 a.m. press conference at the BBC studio had been arranged. I thought it might be like talking to Des Lynam again, but this time the interview took place in one of the small TV rooms in the main Olympic headquarters. I had to go in on my own and talk to an automatic camera, with only an ear-piece connecting me to the main studio in London. All I had to guide me was the voice in my ear. It was the first time I had ever done anything like that, and there I was, live, on breakfast TV!

I met up with Jon and Bruce at lunchtime, first for a photocall, then afterwards to go for a private meal. The photographers were all keen to get shots of Jon and me together, because until he had walked in on the Des Lynam programme the previous evening I think very few journalists had realized Jon existed. Now they had a new angle, and they were making the most of it.

Afterwards, we managed to get away as planned, and found a little restaurant near the Mizuno headquarters. I was still going at 100 m.p.h.! The fact that I had won Olympic gold was at last beginning to sink in, although every now and again I still got jolts of unreality and a feeling of disbelief.

In one of my calmer moments during that lunch I said to Jon, 'You know this is really going to change our lives, don't you?'

'I think it already has,' he replied, but he was grinning.

We talked about this for a while, but at that stage most of our conversation was speculative. I felt very strongly I was on the edge of something unknown.

After lunch, Jon told me he had a TV set in his hotel room, so we went there together, intending to watch John Regis run his heat. We sat down on the edge of the bed about half an hour before the heat was due to begin, but we both fell asleep. The afternoon slipped imperceptibly away.

We slept for a few hours, and when we woke up we were both hungry again. We went back to the village, where I asked the officials if Jon could have a pass. Suddenly, the impossible was within reach! A pass was quickly made out for him.

We didn't feel like a full sit-down meal, so we headed for the McDonald's. The place was packed, but I was spotted immediately! Life had undoubtedly changed for the better. We were immediately found a free table, and the top of it was *cleaned* for us!

Jon went back to England that evening, but I still had the relay to run. With Jon gone, something of the old atmosphere of nervy anticipation returned. Of all the track events, the relay is the one genuine team event, and as team captain I felt I had to do more than just turn up for the race and run. I spent the evening in the Village with the other girls.

The next day I ran in the heat for the relay, and we qualified for the final by coming second. I ran the last leg, but I was still mentally drained by the hurdles win and its aftermath, and I did not run at full power.

The day after we had the relay final, and we went through the same long process of warming up and reporting. I remained tired, but the fact that this was a final gave me the extra spice I needed. By the time we were about to start the race I was ready to go. It was a whole different feeling, a return of the familiar one of wanting to compete at my best.

Because I was again running the last leg, I was able to watch most of the race before I got involved. Phylis Smith ran an excellent first leg at 51.30 seconds; Sandra Douglas ran the second leg at 52.00 seconds. When Jenny Stoute took the baton for the third leg our team was in fourth position, but Jenny had a great run and managed to overtake the Canadian girl in front of her. I took the baton, knowing that the girl in second place was too far ahead to be caught, but determined that I should not relinquish third place. I ran, in fact, my best-ever time of 50.40 seconds, and our British team picked up the bronze medal.

In spite of the furore in Barcelona that had followed my gold medal, I still had no conception of what was going to happen when we got off the plane at Heathrow.

The first hint came after the plane had landed. The cabin crew said that people in the terminal wanted Linford and me to leave the plane by the rear exit (the rest of the team had left by the usual front exit). We came through Customs and Immigration in the normal way, then collected our bags and headed downstairs.

The press were waiting here, and the moment we arrived they all seemed to go mad. It was chaotic. There was a barrage of cameras, microphones and questions. Nothing had prepared me for this! We did the best we could, but once again there was that terrifying feeling of being one person at the mercy of so many. People were calling out to me, and pushing and pressing autograph books into my hands. Meanwhile, what Linford and I really wanted to do was to find the people who had come to the airport to meet us, and go home with them! Linford was being met by all his family, while I knew that Jon's Mum and Dad had come to pick me up. I knew they would be somewhere out there beyond the scrum, but I didn't know how to find them.

They turned up while I was doing the umpteenth TV interview. As soon as I could I told them I was ready, and we made a dash for it. They had parked their car in one of the short-term car parks close to the terminal, and people followed us all the way there, still asking questions about how I felt, what I was going to do next, and all the rest of it.

Once we were away from the immediate vicinity of the airport I felt free of the pressure, and settled back to chat happily with John and Joyce.

As we reached Patcham, though, and drove down the road towards the cottage, my heart sank. Numerous cars were jamming the road, and a small crowd had gathered outside the house. These were reporters from the local press and TV stations, and I was forced to hold more impromptu interviews on the doorstep. I could see my neighbours peering at me.

At last I got into the house, and greeted Jon and my cat, more or less in that order. Jon showed me the pile of letters that had arrived while I was away, and told me that from the moment he had got back into the house the phone had hardly stopped ringing.

One of the invitations waiting for me was from the Lord Mayor of Brighton. He wanted us to go to tea with him at the Pavilion in Brighton that same afternoon, so we did. He put it to me that the corporation would like me to do an open-top bus tour of Brighton, but although I was flattered and knew that it was a kindly invitation I didn't want to do that. I felt I had not really lived in Brighton long enough to have earned it.

This chaotic whirl of events was to continue for a long time. For instance, every day for the two weeks following my return from Spain there was a photo-call of one kind or another. I was still trying to get to meetings to race, and more particularly I still needed to train, but most of this had to go by the board. My time was taken up by one long interview after another, and it seemed that everyone was trying to get a bit of me. Complete strangers would knock on my door late at night, in the hope of catching a little glimpse of Jon or me, or the way we lived.

It was not long before we reached the point when we knew we could not allow this state of affairs to go on much longer. Neither of us was used to such attention. It was great fun, highly flattering, and in fact extremely good to realize the pleasure my win had brought to so many people, but it was slowly destroying the way of life that had led to that win.

On the other hand, I'm a happy-go-lucky person, much given to enjoying myself, and the truth was that I wanted to make the most of it because a large part of me was having fun.

This was a real dilemma and I felt pulled in two directions. I kept thinking someone should be there to tell me what to do, how to handle this or that situation, how to respond to a particular request or invitation. How was everything to be weighed up? But there were no rules about dealing with this kind of thing. When you win a gold medal you are not also given a handbook telling you what to do after you've won. The companies who run football pools have full-time members of staff whose job it is to counsel the big-money winners, and advise them of the best way to protect themselves and build a new future. In a sense, I had won sport's biggest prize, but Jon and I were very much on our own, with no one to tell us what to expect.

What it boiled down to was this: we needed to protect our lifestyle and privacy, and through that protect my ability to train and to keep competing effectively. I was well aware that the season was ending, that winter was approaching. I was already thinking ahead to the following year, and I knew that the winter months were again going to be crucial for training.

Part of the difficulty was that although I wanted to remain approachable, I did need privacy. I knew that if I tried to retreat from the public eye we would upset sections of the press. Both Jon and I had already seen how some newspapers had deliberately set up certain athletes as popular icons, but when something had not gone entirely to plan, had immediately set out to destroy them. In my case, all I had as far as the press was concerned was one big win. They couldn't take that away from me, but if I were to follow it up with a sensational defeat they would probably leap all over me. I knew we were playing a hard game.

Of course, I know now, and have always known, that there will come a day when I don't win, and that eventually I will retire. I accept that. My long-term hope is that by the time that comes around I'll have achieved so much that people will recognize that enough is enough, and that nothing (and nobody) runs forever. But back then, at the end of summer 1992, I felt my hold on success was fragile and that there were forces out there which would be only too glad to remind me of that, given the chance.

Fortunately, I had Jon and his family to keep my feet firmly on the ground. And Jon still kept those turkey photos close at hand, just in case.

Fortunately, too, the month of October was approaching. Jon and I had laid our plans, and were preparing to spend much of that month abroad. There was something we had been planning together for more than a year.

Chapter 15

Florida Gold

In October 1992 we flew out to Florida to get married. There was speculation in the press that we only decided to get married after I had won at the Olympics, but this was not the case.

The subject of marriage first arose when Jon and I were out in Florida on holiday in 1990, at a time when we were living together but had nothing definite for the future fixed up between us. We were in a restaurant, and out of the blue I said to him, 'What about us, then?'

'All right,' he said. 'Why don't we get married?'

I burst into tears on the spot!

Later, we walked back to our hotel. It was about 10.30 p.m., and I wanted Jon to get on the telephone and ring my Dad and ask him, because I wanted to tell everybody. We had made some friends on this holiday and I was desperate to tell them, for a start. Jon had said he wanted to handle the whole thing properly, and wasn't keen for anyone to know until he had asked Dad for his permission. But 10.30 p.m. in Florida is 3.30 a.m. in England, so we thought we had better wait . . .

We spent the next week and a half peering at rings in

jewellers' windows. One day we were over at Pompano Beach, and we saw a couple getting married right there on the sand. We were both rather struck by this. It revealed such a difference between the USA and home. You can't imagine anyone getting married on a beach in England! We both thought, *'Why can't we do that?'*

So that settled it. We decided to get married over there in Florida, on a beach! The only extra we agreed on was that both sets of parents would be there too.

Jon was still determined to do this properly and ask my Dad's permission, so as soon as we were back in England we drove up to see my parents. We arrived at Sunday lunchtime.

Because Dad is a farmer he always gets up at four in the morning, and so he likes to have a little nap in the afternoon. He was asleep when we got there, but I couldn't wait. I pushed Jon towards the living-room where Dad was sleeping.

I said, 'Go on, go in! Get him while he's on his own!'

Poor Jon was so embarrassed, he didn't know what on earth to say. He got halfway through the door, before turning round and coming straight back out.

'Look, if you don't go through with it I'm going to tell him myself!' I said

I think Jon felt awkward about waking Dad up. So I took matters into my own hands. I knocked loudly on the door and pushed Jon through before he could get away.

'Dad, Jon wants to ask you something,' I said.

As my father opened his eyes blearily, Jon said, 'While we were away, if it's all right with you, Sally and I thought we'd like to get engaged.'

Dad pretended to look grumpy.

'Is that all?' he said. 'You woke me up just for that? I don't know about that.'

And then Mum came in, and we all laughed.

With the family formalities out of the way we carried on looking for rings, but we couldn't find what I wanted. Then one day we went to visit Jon's nan, and when we told her about the problem she suddenly got her engagement ring out of a box she kept under her bed. It was rather the worse for wear, but it was lovely! She was as pleased as I was. It did not take long to get it repaired, and I still wear it now. It has an extra-special meaning for me, because of whose it was.

I think my Mum and Dad were a bit shocked when we told them we wanted to marry in the USA, but once we had explained why they were quite happy.

A year passed, and then the Olympics year dawned. We had a few ideas about where in America we would like to get married, but none of the places was quite right. Then, when I was looking through a booklet about Florida, I came across a mention of the South Seas Plantation, on Captiva Island off the west coast of Florida. It sounded perfect, so on our way over to Phoenix, Arizona, for that winter training visit Jon and I flew down to check the place out. It was just as perfect as we had imagined – a private plantation called the King's Lawn, situated at the end of the island. It had a beautiful stretch of grass with palm trees all around and the sea in the background.

We spoke to Ruth Keal, the lady who organized the weddings on the Plantation, and when we told her the sort of ceremony we envisaged having, she simply said that she could arrange it so we did whatever we wanted. For instance, we could write our own service, and make our own promises.

We immediately agreed to get married there, and after the three of us had run through what Jon and I wanted, we left her to arrange it all. With the Olympics coming up I could not afford to expend too much mental energy on organizing our wedding.

Once the Olympics were out of the way we went full steam ahead. Interflora, who were sponsoring me at the time, did all the flowers. Karen Boyd, a girlfriend of Jon's brother Chris, was a designer, and she and I had been working on my dress beforehand. We decided what sort of food and drink we wanted, and faxed all the information to Florida.

Then we had to decide who to invite. We felt this was a bit tricky because, although there seemed to be dozens of people we wanted to ask, we didn't want anyone to feel obliged to pay for a trip to Florida that they couldn't afford just because they felt they had to accept our invitation. What we decided in the end was not to send out the usual formal invitations, but to tell everyone where and when it was going to be held, while letting them know that if they wanted to come they would be more than welcome!

By this time the press had found out we were getting married and wanted to be there to take photos. One of the reasons for sticking to our decision to hold the wedding in America was because we knew most of the press would find it hard to get out there for it! Also, the place itself was in such a remote location that half of them probably wouldn't be able to find it anyway.

As it was, however, we resolved the problem of the press by selling exclusive photographic rights to *Hello!* magazine. Not only did this mean we weren't swamped with dozens of other photographers, it also guaranteed us a terrific set of wedding pictures.

Security remained a minor obsession. The Plantation suggested that our booking and any future communication with them should be made under a false name. They suggested this over the phone, asking for a possible name, on a day that I happened to be watching an old movie. At first I couldn't think of any name, but Marilyn Monroe suddenly appeared on the TV in front of me, so I said 'Monroe'! We then became known as the Monroe wedding . . . to the extent that all the time we were there, my Dad was known as 'Mr Leslie Monroe'.

My Mum and Dad had never flown such a long way before, and had not experienced jet lag, so we took care of them for the first week they were out there. We took them over to the other side of Florida and showed them around, before going on to Captiva Island about three days before the wedding.

The other guests started trickling in soon afterwards. In the end fifty-two people turned up! It was wonderful, just like a big holiday with family and friends. A lot of athletes with whom we're friendly were there: Linford and Colin, Mark McKoy, Sallyanne Short, John Regis and Jenny Stoute, Carmen Smart. Bruce and Julie Longden came too.

We had rented a couple of beach houses, so the night before the wedding we had a hen night and a stag night. The beach houses were so close to each other that we ended up all together in one big party. We girls started our celebrations by going off for a barbecue at the Bubble Restaurant down the road, but we came back and gatecrashed the men's party.

When we woke up in the morning, everyone still seemed to be in the same carefree mood of the night before. One of the great advantages of leaving most of the arrangements to other people is that it's not your worry if they go wrong. In fact, we were so laid back about it all that the organizers at the Plantation began to worry that *we* weren't worried!

I said to them, 'We're all on holiday, so no one's going to care if something goes wrong or doesn't turn up, or it's an hour late. We're here to enjoy ourselves.'

I had been up since 6.30 a.m., when Jon went for a

run. Then we had breakfast with the girls, after which I did my hair and nails and put on my dress (what *Hello!* magazine later described as a sarong-style dress with an off-the-shoulder train). I had my niece Jenny as a bridesmaid, and nephew John as a pageboy. Jon had three best men! (We didn't want anyone to feel obliged to make speeches, and because Jon is really close to his Dad and his brothers Matthew and Chris, he felt that not choosing between them would emphasize the informality of the whole day.)

Dad and I, with my attendants, went down in a sort of van to wait in one of the rooms. There was an unexpected delay as Linford Christie, renowned for his fast getaway on the athletic track, couldn't get his car to start! They had to use one of the other cars, and drive people down in relays.

So twenty minutes later than expected we walked down through the park and up to the middle of the great lawn. I was going too fast, and that made a lot of people laugh. There was a big arch of flowers in the centre of the lawn and a local Justice of the Peace called Gigi Rogers came along to marry us. It was a lovely ceremony. It wasn't the usual 'I do' and promising to obey . . . instead, it was all about love and marriage, what love was really like and what relationships meant. We stood there soaking it all up, while some of the people were crying in the background! Jon was also a bit carried away, and stuttered on his words.

The photographer from the magazine took scores of pictures: from his point of view our wedding was a heaven-sent opportunity, with all these well-known faces acting silly and playing up to the camera. The food was brilliant: there was a huge ice-sculpture in the shape of crossed fishes, and as it melted it helped keep cool the huge platters of oysters, lobster and crab claws. My Uncle Geoff got up and stood on a chair and said a few words, very traditionally. Everyone was relaxed by then. So at the end he told us to go away, and we had a cook-out. It was starting to get really warm outside, so we moved indoors; we were told that we were lucky, that the weather could have been *really* hot at that time of year, but that day there was a breeze blowing in from the Gulf of Mexico. Indoors we got to work on the steaks that now appeared, and drank gallons of champagne.

With the appearance of the cake came more speeches. Dad made a speech, then Jon got up and said a few words. Meanwhile, the athletes, who were all sitting together on one table, had already drawn straws to establish which one of them was going to make a speech. Colin Jackson had drawn the short straw.

As he reached the end of his speech, Colin said, 'Of course, all that now remains for me to do is to hand over to Linford!'

So then Linford had to stand up, and so it went on, around the whole table. When it was Jennifer's turn she was in floods of tears. By the end of it all, I was crying too!

It got round to 3.00 p.m., and the wedding started to lose any vestige of formality. All the men went off, put their swimming trunks on, and climbed onto the Plantation's water-scooters. They roared around on these, trying to burn off a lot of energy. I was wandering around on the beach in my wedding dress, with a video camera, filming all these drunks falling off their scooters in great clouds of spray. In the evening we all went down to Chadwicks' Restaurant for a meal, and carried on celebrating until after 11.00 p.m.

The next day, to our great regret, everyone said their farewells and began leaving. If I could change anything about the wedding I would have booked an extra day afterwards, because I felt the party was only just getting into swing when suddenly it was over. Also, Jon and I had this novel and wonderful feeling that we were *married*, and we wanted everyone to stay around and enjoy more time with us.

When only our families were left with us, we packed our bags and drove across to Disneyworld, where we stayed for three whole days.

Finally, when Jon and I were the last ones left, we set off on our real honeymoon at last: a friend had invited us to join him on his yacht for a cruise through the British Virgin Islands.

Chapter 16

Picking Myself
Up Again

After the wedding there began one of the busiest periods of
my life. It started with the general chaos of a house-move.
The cottage in Patcham, where we had lived since May
1991, was now really too small for us. A few weeks before
the Olympics we had found a larger place, further out of
Brighton, and in November we moved into it.

In many ways, the sheer hell of moving house was as
nothing compared with the hectic life I now found myself
leading. None of the excitement had died down while we
were away, but had, if anything, intensified slightly. I was
in constant demand for public relations work to promote
or support certain products or causes . . . and every mail
delivery seemed to bring ever larger bundles of letters from
ordinary members of the public. All of these things had to
be dealt with somehow.

And, somehow or other, I had to start focusing on the
season ahead. In 1993 the World Championships would be
taking place in Stuttgart, and the cumulative effect of my
performances in the Tokyo World Championships, and then

in the Olympics, meant that I could not afford to miss them. In fact, not only had I no intention whatsoever of missing them, I fully intended to win.

I went to a few meetings at the tail end of the season, between returning from the Olympics and going to Florida. For instance, there is always a welcome-home meeting in Sheffield, after the Olympics. All the medal winners attend this. It's an opportunity to race in front of a home crowd, and have a good time with your friends. It takes place only about a week after the Olympics, so we're all tired, and in my case I was heavily distracted by the after-effects of winning my gold medal. I had been doing PR work all week before the meet. I turned out, though, and was rewarded by everyone in the stadium standing up for me when I went out to race.

The funny thing is that this race, which should have been easy, served as a reminder of the need to keep my mind on my running, because I only just won! One of the British girls went bombing off at the start, and I had my work cut out to catch her up. Luckily, I was able to come through at the end.

There was a big meeting in Zürich shortly after the one in Sheffield, and it was here I suffered an injury to my hamstring. This has become a fairly regular problem which never seems to get any worse, but at the time I felt it was enough of a warning and I decided to call it a day after that.

I started training again in November, whilst also facing a storm of new commitments. It was all so new to me, and although I was happy doing it I found it impossible to be sure I wasn't doing too much of the PR work and not enough of the training.

Everyone around me, the people close to me who care, was saying, 'Don't forget your training.'

Even though I know I was doing the training I was still

panicking about it. Every time I went out to do some it was in the aftermath of a trip to London, or an appearance on TV, or a hurried flight up to Scotland, or something like that; and while I was actually training my mind would be on the next job I had to do, the next commitment in the diary.

I was torn between the demands of the two. I wanted to do both. I was happier with my life than I had ever been before, and felt not only busy but productively busy. I was also training hard. But I knew then, and know now, that I would not be able to sustain that sort of pressure forever.

Another problem was that during this period Jon was still working full-time at his job in London, so that for much of the time I was working on my own. This meant that there were many occasions when I was away, staying in a hotel somewhere on my own, and in circumstances like these training is difficult for me.

Then there was the uncomfortable but undeniable fact that some of the PR appearances I was being called upon to do turned out to be fairly boring or irritating; two responses to which I am fairly vulnerable. If I had Jon with me nothing like this mattered, but sometimes it was undeniably tough when I was on my own.

The good thing, the really positive thing, was that having the PR work to do made me see the training in a different light. Because it threatened the training, ironically the PR work made me value it more.

I was forced into the realization that I still wanted to train, to race, and ultimately to win. All these distractions were motivating me again.

We returned to Florida in January, this time to the capital Tallahassee in the north of the state, where I embarked on the hardest three weeks of training in my life. It was just Jon and myself. We had originally been planning to go to

159

South Africa, where Bruce was doing a coaching course, but in the end it began to seem politically threatening down there. There were attempts to get us involved in what turned out to be a predominantly white group, but half our training group is black. We pulled out at the last minute. I still needed warm-weather training, though, so we chose Florida again.

In effect, I used those three weeks to change a negative into a positive. A lot of people had been asking me how I was going to pick myself up after the Olympics and focus on the World Championships; they meant well, but the question implied a negative. I had to go to Florida to find the positive answer for myself.

When we came back to England, I had no trouble in focusing on the World Championships, and the question had been answered.

After our return I ran as usual at a couple of indoor meetings. I had set myself the target of breaking 52 seconds for the 400m flat, but although I won all three races, one in the Belgian town of Ghent, the other two in England, I didn't manage to reach that target. 52.35 seconds was the best I could do, and I had to be satisfied with that.

I see the indoor events in February and March as part of my winter training; they are a good opportunity to get out and see how I can race after strength training. Speed training comes later.

In March, I went away with Bruce and the rest of the girls to Las Palmas in the Canary Islands. The weather wasn't too good, which was a slight disappointment, as the chief reason for these winter trips is to find warm weather in which to train. In addition, we were staying in a hotel right in the middle of town, so there was nowhere to run around in the immediate locality. To do any kind of training we had to pile into the van and head off. However, the track we were using was fine. There was also a golf course about twenty minutes away, which pleased both Bruce and myself.

For me, the purpose of this trip was to get back to the 400m hurdles again, because up to this point I'd only been concentrating on the running side of it. The March trips are really for going into technique work and stride pattern. It's usually a bit warmer by this time of year, so the work is a lot easier to do then.

After a few days the weather improved, and we had some really good track sessions. We also had quite a laugh. I was sharing with Jenny again, and often it was just as though we were back in the old times.

We returned to England during the last week in March, and I concentrated on training in April and spent it at home with Jon. I cut down heavily on the PR work; the summer season was getting ever closer.

In May I went away again for two weeks, this time to Portugal, with the usual group. Now I was starting my speed training. As ever, I really missed Jon during this trip. It's psychologically a difficult time, because I'm finding out if I have done enough training. It's also a time when I begin to have doubts about whether I'm going to be fit enough for the season. This trip was really the last opportunity to find these things out, and still have a chance to put them right.

It's a good sign to worry about these things! But the worry can be a torment, because if I can't get my form right before the racing begins I probably never will.

The first race I ran that year was at the relay meeting in Portsmouth, and I immediately ran the fastest relay leg I've ever done. I knew from that I was in good shape. Jenny Stoute was running well and feeling high too.

But there can be a downside to this too: it's always possible to run too fast too early, so if you find yourself thinking that you're doing that you try and steady up a bit.

In the UK Championships I ran a 200m flat race, and came up against a young athlete called Katharine Merry. She ran a hard race and beat me into second place. A lot of newspapers leapt on that, with headlines such as 'Olympic Champion Beaten by Youngster', and so on. As far as I was concerned I had run a personal best, which was what I had been aiming for, and I was pleased about that. In any case it's her event, not mine; she is number 1 in the country, so I wasn't particularly bothered about the result. It presumably gave Katharine quite a boost, too.

I gave myself a boost soon afterwards, when I went out and did my first 400m hurdles at the Rome Grand Prix meeting. I felt nervous about this race simply because it was the first 400m hurdles of the year, and many of my rivals were there. Not Sandra Farmer-Patrick, though. I won the race in 54.64 seconds, which was good and fast, and which pleased me. The runner-up was Deon Hemmings from Jamaica, who had been another finalist in Barcelona.

The following week I was back in Rome again, this time for the Europa Cup. In this each country is represented by one person per event. Britain was in the 'A' Division, so we had the hardest draw, and I was not only in the first event, the 400m hurdles, but also in the last one, the relay. This is the only meet where you're really needed as a Captain. Each team is small and firmly identified as running for the country, so each competitor has a strong sense of identity with the other athletes in her team.

I felt that the pressure was on me, then, to go out there and set a good example from the outset.

The draw put me in Lane 8, which seemed like a bad omen, but I ran really well. I had a Russian girl catching me up at the eighth hurdle, but I pulled away from her at the end. I ran a time of 53.73 seconds. To dip beneath 54 seconds so early in the season was exciting.

After the Europa Cup the season settled down into the usual round of Grands Prix (mostly abroad), and races at home. The Grand Prix meeting in Lausanne was the first competition that year in which I ran against Sandra Farmer-Patrick. The organizers built it up as the highlight of the meet, a clash between us. I went out and won it in pretty good time, well under 54 seconds.

Sandra then disappeared from the scene, claiming she was injured. I won all of my next few races, in Nice and Zürich, and the TSB Games at Crystal Palace. This last race was a hard one. As we came down the back straight it started to rain, and we had to run into a headwind and lashing rain on the home straight. I came in at 53.80 seconds, twenty metres clear.

With the sole exception of that 200m flat, I won every single race in the weeks leading up to the World Championships. I was also winning them with a big distance between me and the runner-up, so you can imagine the pressure was building up on me.

With only two or three weeks to go before the World Championships, we had one last meeting in Zürich, then moved to a holding camp about an hour away from Zürich, in a small town called Zofingen. Bruce was there to work with me, but all the other athletes who were intending to compete in the Championships were also there.

I moved into the final stages of my preparations.

Earlier in the year I had started working with a nutritionist called Eric Llewelyn. I grew interested in the subject of nutrition when I started thinking about how I could boost my attempt to win the World Championships by finding those extra percentages. At the top levels of sport the margins are so tiny! I thought I was eating cautiously, and therefore well, but I realized my diet could probably be better and I thought this might be an area on which I could work.

Most nutritionists begin by listing what you would normally eat during a day. Eric Llewelyn's method was to ask me what kinds of food I really craved. I told him my favourite food was Chinese. Next he asked me what I really hated. I said cabbage, broccoli, green vegetables . . . I've never been very keen on vegetables! Eric wrote all this down. Then he asked me which was my favourite fruit, and which was the one I hated most. Next he went through starchy foods like bread and biscuits, asking what I really loved, and what were the embarrassments. I said potato crisps. I really love crisps! On he went, through every kind of food.

When I next saw him he had worked out a diet for me, one that was based on energy production. The idea behind it was to eat as many natural foods as possible. Free-range chicken and fish. Organic vegetables were ideal. Every time the body is trying to break down something it uses up energy. He recommended that I eat foods which are natural, as free as possible of preservatives and flavourings, that the body could recognize and absorb quickly. I also had to drink six pints of water a day, to cleanse the body, and to cut out tea and coffee. He prescribed starting the day with both a cold shower (which I was already doing) to detoxify the body, and a drink of lemon with hot water and honey. I was allowed to carry on with the stir-fried food I enjoyed eating so much, and at lunchtime I could have simple meals like baked beans on jacket potatoes. The main idea was to eat fresh food which contained no preservatives. In essence, he was saying, 'If you want something, have it.'

I tried cutting down on convenience food, and followed his advice for a while, but then I began to suffer cravings. For instance, I began lusting after chips and other fatty foods. And chocolate! How I was missing chocolate!

When I saw Eric again, he simply said, 'If that's the case, have it.' His point was that this was not a diet to make me lose weight, but to create physical energy.

I started the diet in earnest in March 1993, and I can honestly say that within the first two weeks I noticed the difference. I was more alert. I woke up in the mornings feeling better. Recovery from exercise was quicker. They were all small things, but they made me feel as if I was a totally different person. I couldn't believe it.

Because these effects were so noticeable, I made myself follow the diet more strictly as the World Championships approached. Diets are infinitely more easy to obey if you have a clearly defined target and a deadline.

The diet meant that I was creating energy so I could train that little bit harder. Without the diet, an evening session might tire me after ten minutes, but with it I could probably train a bit harder for fifteen minutes.

I also now have my own physiotherapist, Kim Wurmli. I had been consulting Kim in a general way in Brighton once a week for about four years. I would always see her even if I was not injured, and she would give me a general massage or a Thai massage. (A Thai massage involves the use of the body's pressure points to make the body supple.) When we went to Zofingen I asked Kim to be there too. If you are going to get injured, inevitably it will always be in the week before a major event! I managed to get her on to the Mizuno team for the World Championships, and they paid her hotel expenses.

We had a week of intense training in Zofingen. This means it was not physically hard, but we were putting the final sessions together, the final speed work.

But then something went wrong. There was a cold going

around, and halfway through the week I discovered I had caught it. I tried not to panic, because at that time I was doing a couple of my sessions, which were going quite well. I didn't want to give in to it. At any other time of the year I probably would have pulled out of some of the training sessions, but then, just a few days before the World Championships, I couldn't even consider it. All I could do was try not to think too much about it.

I rang up my nutritionist and he immediately gave me a list of things to inhale, and stuff to put in my bath water. He also told me to drink as much thyme tea as possible. I tried this once, but it was revolting! It made me sick, and did absolutely nothing for my cold.

When the day came we all drove up to Stuttgart in hired cars. My throat was rasping, my nose was blocked, and I had a terrible hacking cough. I wanted to be in bed, not on the way to the toughest race of my career!

Chapter 17

World Gold – and the Future

We found the athletes' village in Stuttgart, obtained our accreditation and checked in. As we had done so often before, we arrived as late as legitimately possible, to minimize the time spent hanging around before the event. Partly because of this, and partly because we did not check in as a team, we ran into administrative problems with checking in, but these were eventually sorted out.

We were taken across to our dormitories. We couldn't believe the accommodation we were shown! The village appeared to have once been an army barracks: the beds were made of wooden battens and the mattresses were only about an inch thick. Once again we were allocated one room between two people, so I shared with Jenny again. We were lucky, because in many cases four people were sharing one room.

The rest of the accommodation was as spartan as the beds: the kitchen, for instance, had no utensils or cooking implements. The lounge area consisted of bare floorboards, on which two wooden chairs faced a television set. This meant that if all four of us in the apartment wanted to watch one of the events, two of us would have to sit on the floor. As it happened, the television coverage of the athletics was patchy, so it was difficult anyway to remain aware of what was going on at the track. But the food was so awful that a couple of people went down with food poisoning.

The one aspect of this that really got to me was that the IAAF was making millions of dollars out of the championships, yet they made us stay in a dump like this! They couldn't even give us decent accommodation.

The Americans must have felt the same way, because after a brief conference the whole lot of them moved out and found hotels! I thought long and hard about doing the same, but to take part fully in a big meet like this you have to get into the atmosphere, take things as they come. And I was the women's captain. I talked to Linford, the men's captain, and he said he felt he had to set an example.

However, I was now in contact with Jon, who was undecided about whether or not to fly to Stuttgart to watch me race. I said to him, 'I think it might be worthwhile if you could come over and find a hotel room. Then I could join up with you if I need to get a good night's sleep.' (We were being woken up at all hours in the village.) Jon came out to Germany on the day I did my heats.

Everything was being made much worse for me by my cold, which had developed into a beauty! I was trying to keep my concern about it to myself, not wanting to look as if I was preparing excuses, but in truth it was making me feel terrible. You really do feel an internal pressure to keep quiet about it if you catch a cold. You don't even want other people in your team to know. In the end I went to see the team doctor, and he said maybe I should take some antibiotics. I was nervous that they might affect my performance, so he suggested that I go on a short intensive course for three days, then have two days completely free of them before the race.

Bruce was unhappy about this, and went to talk to the doctor too. Afterwards, he said to me, 'OK, but make sure you're off them when the doctor said.'

Once I had begun the course of antibiotics I did start feeling better, especially as I was about to do some racing. I spent a fair bit of time at the hotel being used by Mizuno, so I had somewhere to escape to briefly, and, perhaps even more important, to eat some decent food. Kim, my physiotherapist, was also there, because of her connection with the Mizuno team, and one of her massages always makes me feel better.

I had been drawn to run in Heat 1, Lane 3. I brightened at this news.

In keeping with the rest of the arrangements, the bus service down to the stadium was horrible; it was a long way and I had to stand. All the way along I was dying to cough, but because some of the girls I would be running against were on the same bus I did not dare to let it go. You find yourself tensing and working your throat, swallowing a lot, making funny noises. When they finally dropped us off it was right in front of the stadium itself, so we had to walk past the crowds to get into the warm-up area.

Once inside, though, I felt myself clicking into gear. Negatives turned to positive. I thought, *'At least today I'm going to find out how I really am!'*

Everyone seemed to be there in the warm-up area, medical teams and managers, as well as the athletes. Bruce was there, of course, in charge of the heptathletes. I found myself my usual little place with a bit of shade and sat down there. Bruce eventually came along to see me.

We chatted for a little while, but Bruce is really very good at noticing when I don't want to talk. He knew I was suffering with my cold, but he didn't keep asking me how I was, how I felt, and unhelpful questions like that. He simply ascertained that I was fit to run, and that I wanted to run, and that was good enough for him.

When we had checked in, we were led into the stadium by a most bizarre access route: a temporary scaffolding bridge had been built between the warm-up area and the stadium itself. We had to climb up about thirty steps, then cross the bridge, which was rocking all over the place with the vibrations of our steps. I was at the back of the line, so I felt this more than the others did. After the bridge we had to go down the other side, then along another flight of steps, winding endlessly upwards. When we emerged into the daylight we were right at the top of the stadium with all the crowds below us. We were taken to a room and told to wait until we were called.

After we had been checked for kit, spikes, numbers and (Germanic thoroughness) against a photograph, there was a chance to go to the loo. I dived thankfully in. At last I had a chance to have a good cough, and to blow my nose! I was thinking, 'How am I even going to get round?'

I was subsiding into negative thoughts, not at all like my usual self. I was thinking I could collapse on, say, the seventh hurdle. Or I could cross the line and have a coughing fit. I was really worried about that! At this late stage all I could do was run the race and see what might happen. The only alternative would have been to scratch, to pull out of the race altogether.

When we were finally called we walked down a lot more steps, and came out at the side of the track by the second hurdle. From here we had to walk back around the first bend to get to the start. We were still early, and there were a couple of races that had to be run before ours. I found myself a little bit of shade by a wall, and I just lay there with my legs up on the wall. I looked across the stadium once, and saw Sandra coming out for her own heat.

They took us out about five minutes before the heat was due to start, which was fine by me. The less hanging around we do at the start the better I like it. I had a quick run over the hurdles, and realized my body was in good shape. It was early in the morning, and the sun was still relatively low, so the stadium wasn't particularly full and there wasn't much atmosphere.

The gun went and we got away first time.

Running down the back straight I was thinking, *'How am I feeling? Am I breathing too hard? Am I OK?'*

Apart from the cold I felt good, but I made quite a few mistakes over the hurdles. I wasn't feeling positive enough to attack them properly. I kept thinking about how I was feeling.

But I came across the line first, and my first thought was that I was OK. I looked across at the time, and it was 55.07 seconds. It was good enough to win, but it was in fact the slowest I ran all year.

As I was recovering I realized that I didn't seem to be spluttering. There were some press guys there as usual, and they asked me how I was feeling. They obviously didn't know about the cold, and I didn't want to tell them. So I said, 'Well, I'll talk to you later'. Most of the press now know that I prefer not to talk to them until after the final, when I'll give them as much time as they like. They accept this, and so these guys simply said 'OK', and we left it at that.

I had a massage with Kim at the Mizuno place, and then went for dinner with Jon. In their different ways, both worked their magic and I began to feel better, and more optimistic, about the semifinal the next day.

I had an early night at the village, sitting on my bed talking to Jenny. She had her own problems with an injury and wasn't sure whether she should run the next day. I eventually lay down on my fiendishly uncomfortable bed, and fell asleep while still coughing and spluttering.

The semifinal the next day was at 7.30 p.m. I went down on the bus again, this time with the British 400m hurdlers Gowry Retchakan and Jacqui Parker, both of whom had got through to the semifinal. Fortunately, they were not in the same semi as I was, and, although we did not say much to each other, it was a relief not to have to avoid eye-contact at all costs!

I was in the first semifinal, while Sandra Farmer-Patrick was in the second. Once again I had come through to quite an easy semi.

Before I left the warm-up area, Bruce made his usual comment.

'Remember that you're not just running to win,' he said. 'You're trying to get a good lane in the final.'

I had been allocated Lane 6 for the semi, and we went off on the gun.

After most races I can't remember much about them, but this one remains clear in my mind. It means, it must mean, that I wasn't focusing enough, and I was therefore not at my best. I made a mistake on the seventh hurdle, the one where I usually change down, but I carried on, pushing all the way. I won, and came in at 53.95 seconds. I was happy with that.

I went and put on my kit, and there was a TV screen within view. The second semifinal was being run, and I wanted to watch but didn't want to watch, if my meaning is clear! I ended up looking at the screen out of the corner of my eye.

I was actually interested to see what sort of shape Sandra

was in. I knew that she had not run all that well in her heat, and had only just got through to the semifinal. There were still rumours of an injury, although I could see she was not wearing bandages or straps.

She ran her semifinal a lot better, and came in second behind Margarita Ponomaryova. Both of them turned in quicker times than mine, which meant that I would be going into the final as only the third fastest.

This was rather different from the situation at the Olympics, and made me seem more of an outsider. I felt I could draw positive thoughts from that.

What in fact I derived from the situation was this: *'I've got a day's rest, I made a mistake, so I know I can run faster than that.'* In absolute terms I wasn't that far behind these girls (I was only .24 of a second behind Ponomaryova's time). And I felt that Sandra had probably been pushed hard enough in her semi to have been running flat out.

The next day was a rest day for me, so that night I stayed the night with Jon in his hotel.

On the evening before the final I was sitting with Jon in the canteen in the village, when Linford Christie and Colin Jackson came in. They sat down with us and started chatting. I was getting nervous about the race the next day, and they quickly sensed that. Without seeming to force it, the two of them launched into a confidence-boosting session for my benefit. They were absolutely unbelievable.

'You can do it!' they said. 'You know you're the best one out there.'

Linford said, 'Look, when we get back to the airport, do you really want me to go through at the front, with you just hanging around in the background with everyone else?'

They kept at it for about an hour and a half, giving me this kind of positive talk. I came out of it feeling completely different, that I could really do it. Even Jon was believing it; I think he was ready to put his spikes on and run the race with me!

I walked with Jon down to his bus, before he went back to the hotel.

When I got up the next day I went straight downstairs to find out the lane draw. For this race it was crucial. If they had put me in Lane 6 I would have panicked. The system works like this: the four semifinalists with the fastest times go into a draw for the four best lanes: 3, 4, 5 and 6. The other four then have their own draw for Lanes 1, 2, 7 or 8.

I saw straight away that I had drawn Lane 4, which was exactly the one I wanted. Sandra Farmer-Patrick was in Lane 6, which was, if anything, even better. This meant that she had no one to watch. Between us, in Lane 5, was Margarita Ponomaryova, so I had someone to chase, and just on my inside was Deon Hemmings.

The day dragged slowly by. When I reached the warm-up area I found that Bruce was already there, and had bagged me my usual bit of shade. I did my warm-up. But I was feeling different this time!

I was doing a lot of talking to myself, and when I walked around I found I was making myself seem tall and aggressive. At one point I went past where Sandra was lying down doing some stretching, and I practically swaggered past her as if I had no cares in the world. It was a totally different me, because I'm really not like that! The thing was, it wasn't aimed at her, a deliberate psyching-out of a rival, it was all directed internally. It was my way of telling myself I could do it. As I did my strides, as I was going over the hurdles, real confidence was brimming out of me. But it was all a façade, put on for the benefit of myself, not aimed at others.

When we were waiting during the check-in I was aware

of Sandra without looking at her, and I was thinking, '*This is going to be close.*' I was certain I could beat her, but I felt that my cold was going to take the edge off my performance.

There seemed to be even more waiting around this time than before. They made us stand for about twenty minutes in the tunnel that led into the stadium while we waited to go out. I was coughing there; I couldn't stop myself! I was still trying to hold the coughs back, but in that draughty, confined space I couldn't help myself. I just hoped the others had their own problems and weren't taking too much notice of me.

As we were led out to the starting blocks, I tried to take note of the crowd without actually looking at them. From the corner of my eye it seemed there were noticeably more British flags than American! Most of the British seemed to have clustered close to the finishing line. I heard my name being shouted. That gave me a boost!

I had my usual practice run over the first hurdle, then came back and sat on the box. We only had to wait about two minutes this time, and the next thing I knew we were on our marks. I was happy about that!

The stadium went all quiet. The starter checked that we were all positioned correctly.

'Set!'

I could feel myself shaking. I was telling myself, '*Right you can do this, you can win this, you can run whatever it takes to win this, believe in yourself.*'

Then the gun went and we got away first time.

I don't remember everything about the race. I remember the second hurdle because I felt a little uneven there, didn't attack it quite right, and felt a little unbalanced.

I said to myself, 'Right, get back into it and relax.'

I remember getting the hurdles right round the bottom bend, and thinking, 'Good, you've got it, go for it!'

175

I came off the eighth hurdle and Sandra was in the lead, but I knew I could get her!

I closed up on her a bit as we went over the ninth, and closed up a bit more on the tenth. Sandra was still slightly in the lead as we hit the ground, – she's always fast on the flat, the hurdling is the weakest part of her race – but I was looking straight ahead, knowing she was there but not knowing how close she was or anything at all . . . and then I was just going and going and *going* for the line.

It was like a slow-motion film again, going for the line. I dived forward, thrusting my chest out.

I crossed the line, and I didn't know whether I had won or not.

I was so focused on getting across that line that I didn't look for Sandra, didn't even know where she was. If you watch a videotape of the finish you can see that I'd won, but at that exact moment, down there in the real world, I didn't know that.

I crossed the line and I didn't know what to do!

There were all these people shouting and cheering, but I didn't know who they were shouting for! What had happened? Did Sandra win? Did I? There was no one there who would say anything, they were all just looking at me and clapping.

Then I must have seen the British flags in front of me. The fans were standing up, cheering and going wild. I realized that I'd done it.

The feeling of relief was stronger than anything else. I couldn't believe that I'd done it, that it was over.

And I was told it was a record, but somehow it didn't sink in that *I* had broken the record. I knew the old record was 52.94 seconds, and they said the race had been won in

52.74 seconds, but for some reason I thought that meant that I had equalled the record.

I didn't care about the record. I had won. That was all that mattered.

Once again I felt myself to be wrapped in a cocoon. I felt cut off from the world outside, numbed by disbelief. I kept trying to take my success in, but nothing made sense to me.

I jogged around my lap of honour. I didn't see Mum and Dad this time, but I got hold of a British flag and all of a sudden a thousand camera shutters clattered around me. There were more press men around me than ever before. I couldn't get past them. I was trying to jog and they were right in front of me! I couldn't get close to the crowd because of them. But when I reached the eighth hurdle I saw my brother Paul, who was standing near there and who gave me a big kiss through a hole in the railings. A little further along the railings were a bit more broken, and here Jon had pushed his way down to the edge. I went up and gave him the biggest hug, and tried to put out of my mind the huge huddle of photographers around us.

I finally left Jon and went up to the big area where the British supporters were gathered. I simply stood there in front of them, trying to convey by grinning at them and waving my flag that I was thanking them. It was they who had made me carry on, and not give up at the end.

There was another line of cameras, and beyond them I saw Sandra again. She had collapsed by the cameras and pulled herself up against the railings. I wasn't quite sure what had happened to her but, to be honest, at that moment I really didn't care!

I went up to the British TV crews and had a long chat with them there on the side of the track. I didn't mention my cold, because all of a sudden that wasn't bothering me any more. I talked about how excited I was, how thrilled I was that I'd been able to equal the world record.

American TV was next; they managed to get Sandra over to their cameras, and they interviewed us side by side. All this was happening in a whirl, without my having any time to think about what was going on. It wasn't as bad as it might have been at some other time, but neither of us had had a chance to think. I said my win was all down to this lady, and running against her had made me able to run such a fast time. When Sandra spoke she kept going on about the fact that *she* had broken the world record too! By this time I'd been able to glimpse the times on the board, and she had come in at 52.78 seconds, just .04 of a second behind me. We had both cracked the record, but she did not want it to be forgotten that she had too. If I had been in her position, that stuff about the world record wouldn't have meant anything. (But, to be fair, I don't know how I would react in that situation.)

I went out to the medal ceremony. One of the team managers was with me, and she kept hugging me. I couldn't think why. Then she said, 'Do you realize you've knocked two-tenths of a second off the world record?'

'Yeah,' I said. Somehow it still didn't register. I thought she was telling me, like everyone was telling me, that I had equalled the old one.

I was looking forward to the ceremony, knowing from the Olympics a little of what to expect. I walked out there, and took the rostrum, and everyone was cheering. I waited for them to announce my name, because that came next. Unreality began to wrap itself insidiously around me. On the loudspeakers, echoing across the stadium, and seeming to echo across the whole city, the voice said, 'Sally Gunnell of Great Britain – gold medal, and new world-record holder!'

The Union Jack was raised, the National Anthem played, and afterwards the crowd went wild.

Then it sank in.

With the ceremony behind us, the three of us were taken to an official press conference. I sat down in the centre, with Sandra to my right and Margarita to my left. We began to field the questions that shot at us, and we went over the ground that was rapidly becoming familiar. We heard about Sandra's world record again, even though she felt the best person had won. When I had my turn I let on at last about my cold, and quite a few of the British press guys picked up on that. As soon as I mentioned it, I rather regretted having done so. I still didn't want to go into it there, because even then I has anxious not to seem to be making excuses.

I noticed that Jon was standing at the back, by the door, and was talking earnestly to a woman who had come in and stood beside him. They were both glancing in my direction.

Shortly, the woman moved away, and Jon weaved through the crowd of reporters and came up to me.

'What was all that about?' I whispered.

'She was from the dope centre. You've only got about five minutes left to get down there, otherwise the record won't stand!'

'What do I do?' I said, looking at the massed ranks of pressmen.

'Get there quick!' Jon said.

Without saying anything, I slipped away from the press conference, and Jon and I hurried down to the drugs testing centre. One of the doctors looked at his watch as we rushed in, then asked me my name. He wrote it down and put the time beside it. One of the officials ticked my name off a list on a clipboard.

I looked over at the long queue; there were only two cubicles and the queue was moving extremely slowly. No one seemed to be in a hurry to get in there. I was in no hurry to get in there either. I was dry!

I felt something cold touch my hand, and I turned. Jon was standing there, holding two just-opened bottles of German beer, glistening with condensation. He passed one to me.

'Cheers!' he said.

'Cheers!' I replied, laughing.

I put the bottle to my lips, and let the delicious golden beer pour helpfully down my throat. It was going to be all right.

Epilogue

What does an athlete do after she has just broken the world record?

I can't speak for everyone, but that night Jon and I went back to my room in the village. Jenny Stoute was there. While I had been in Zofingen I had bought an immense bar of Swiss chocolate. I now took this out of my bag, laid it on the bed, and said, 'Right, here goes!'

The three of us scoffed the lot. A little later, feeling a bit sick, we went down to the canteen and drank some tea. We didn't get much sleep that night . . .

This is the end of my story, and in these closing pages I want to describe how I see my future from my present standpoint in early 1994.

I say without complaint or apology that I have to work for a living, and because I now have to plan for what I'm going to do when I eventually retire, in recent months I have been exploring ways of lending my name to various long-term projects.

When I first came back from the Olympics I began an exhausting round of PR work. This mostly consisted of making an appearance somewhere to give a boost to somebody's cause or product, and although a lot of it was a great deal of fun, some of it began to get me down. I have been saying 'No' more frequently in recent months, preferring to find work that is satisfying to me.

Top of the list must come my connection with the Avon cosmetic company. They are major sponsors of the Breakthrough Breast Cancer Campaign, and they promote what they call Challenge Weekends: tough outdoor pioneer courses, in which volunteers undertake to raise money in their locality spending a weekend – often one that turns out cold and wet, though even so, rewarding and healthy – clambering around in forests and on mountains. I go along to cheer everyone up and give what assistance I can.

Avon are also launching a range of sportswear under my name, which is the first time a woman athlete in this country has lent her name to such a product. I have, in addition, made a promotional video for exercise equipment made by the Forza company, and this video is likely to be the first of several. Later in 1994 I will be presenting my first TV show, called *Bodyheat*, which will be a quest to find the fittest man and woman in Britain. And, still on the theme of personal fitness, I have already laid plans to launch a range of vitamins.

After I won the World Championship I agreed to hold a press conference the next morning. Perhaps unsurprisingly it was mostly the British journalists who turned up.

Journalists, like everyone else, get fed up with going over the same ground twice or more. They had already written about Sally-the-girl-next-door. They had done Sally-the-gold-medallist. They had done Sally-and-Jon-the-happy-couple. Now they had a new agenda for me – and it was one for which I was completely unprepared.

They were interested in money, and from the first question this was the only subject that they wanted to talk about. Did I earn as much money as Linford Christie, they asked. (Linford had also won a gold in Stuttgart.) I hadn't even thought about this! I had no idea what Linford earned, although I imagined it was quite a lot. I said something to that effect. Then another question slammed in: did I think it was fair that he was earning twice as much as I was?

I said, 'Well, we've both won our races, and we both hold Olympic gold, so yes . . . it would be nice to be paid as much as Linford.'

And this was how it started.

Next day, the headlines in the British newspapers said, *'Sally Demands Same Pay as Linford Christie!'*

It's interesting to me how the press can sometimes sense a story, then bring it into the open. Until this point I had never given much serious thought to the differential in pay between male and female athletes; suddenly I was in the forefront of what appeared to be a campaign.

For the first years of my career I needed to be subsidized, either by living at home with my parents, or by taking on part-time jobs, or else by finding what sponsorship or appearance fees I could. When I won the Olympics, and only then, I was able for the first time in my life to command decent fees for what I was doing. That was in 1992, when I was twenty-six years old.

How long does an athlete's career last? I feel that at present I am in peak condition, with perhaps my best performances to come. But time is not on my side, and certainly by the time I am in my early thirties I won't be able to compete at the same level. So, to put it bluntly, I have five years in which I have to earn a lifetime's money!

If I were a man, it would not be fundamentally different, but my ability to earn a living would be spread over a longer period of time, and the individual rewards would be that much greater.

To put it bluntly, I had to be good enough to win an Olympic gold medal before I even came close to making the same kind of money as Linford was already making. Even now, like most top male athletes, he still earns much more than I do.

The significant point, though, is not about Linford and me, or indeed about any athletes who win gold medals. The point is that the vast majority of athletes can barely afford to live, and the women are worse off than the men. If my stance on this will eventually help the young athletes who are coming up behind me, then it will have been worth speaking out in public.

I can never plan too far ahead, when I try to think about what competitions I might enter in the future. There are too many random factors, such as the ever-present risk of injury, to lay firm plans. I have always taken one season at a time, starting to prepare for the next one as the present one ends.

The big challenge for me in 1994 is going to be the European Championships in Helsinki, in which I shall again be running the 400m hurdles.

Almost immediately after that we have the Commonwealth Games in Vancouver. The closeness of these two meetings in time, and the distance between them in terms of miles, is going to be a problem for many athletes. Many of us will be suffering from jet lag as the Games open! While not trying to plan too far ahead, I am currently thinking I might like to run in the 100m hurdles in Vancouver, as well as in my two usual events.

In 1995 there will be another World Championships, and in the year after that, of course, the Atlanta Olympic Games will be held. I want to compete in both of these, but for the time being they are too far away for me to make firm plans.

Retirement? I hope I can continue until at least the Atlanta Olympics, but the real test for me is whether or not I can go on enjoying myself. I have always said, and meant, that when the pleasure leaves running, I shall leave too.

One of the questions I am most frequently asked is about my world record, and whether I think I can break it again. As I hope this book has made clear, records are not the main reason I run, although being the current world record holder does put a slightly different aspect on the subject.

I believe my record is one I can break, and I think will probably do so. If I have an aim, it would be to take the time for the 400m hurdles below 52 seconds.

However, having said this, I would hope that such a time will come not as an end in itself, but as the consequence of running a good race, a perfect race. How is a perfect race defined?

It is one, quite simply, where I get my strides right and take each hurdle perfectly. It is one where the track is right, and the weather is right. It is one where I have competitive rivals who are all on form and keen to beat me. And it is one where there is a terrific crowd watching.

If I can win such a race, it will be in itself much more important to me than a mere entry in a record book.

You may take it that I fully intend to run a perfect race at least once in the months and years that lie ahead.

Fact File

Born: Chigwell (Essex), 29 July 1966
Height: 1.67m (5ft 6in)
Weight: 57kg (9st)
Club: Essex Ladies
Coach: Bruce Longden

Personal Bests

100m	11.83	(1990)
100m	11.79 wind assisted	(1986)
100m hurdles	12.82	(1988 UK record)
100m hurdles	12.80 wind assisted	(1988)
200m	23.30	(1993)
300m	36.44	(1993)
400m	51.11	(1991)
400m	49.46 relay leg	(1991)
400m hurdles	52.74	(1993)
High jump	1.67	(1983)
Long jump	6.08	(1983)

Shot put	11.18	(1984)
Heptathlon	5493	(1984)

Indoor Bests

60m hurdles	8.27	(1987)
200m	24.12	(1989)
400m	51.72	(1994 UK record)
800m	2.0836	(1991)

Career Highlights

1980   1st WAAA Junior Long Jump
1st English Schools Junior Long Jump

1981   1st WAAA Intermediate Long Jump

1983   Semi-finalist European Junior 100m hurdles
13th European Junior Heptathlon
1st English Schools Senior 100m hurdles

1984   Made GB senior debut
1st English Schools Senior 100m hurdles
Set UK Junior record for 100m hurdles of 13.30
(this record still stands)

1986   1st UK Championships and WAAA 100m hurdles
1st Commonwealth 100m hurdles
Eliminated in the heats for the European 100m
hurdles

1987   1st WAAA Indoor 200m hurdles
Eliminated in the heats for the European Indoor 60m
hurdles
1st WAAA 100m hurdles
Semi-finalist World Championships 100m hurdles

1988   1st WAAA Indoor 400m hurdles
4th European Indoor 400m
1st WAAA 100m hurdles and 400m hurdles
5th Olympic 400m hurdles
Semi-finalist Olympic 100m hurdles
Set UK records for 100m hurdles and 400m hurdles

1989   1st European Indoor 400m
6th World Indoor 400m
2nd Europa Cup 400m hurdles
1st WAAA 100m hurdles
3rd World Cup 400m hurdles

1990   1st Commonwealth 400m hurdles (1st 4x400)
2nd Commonwealth 100m hurdles
4th European Indoor 400m
6th European 400m hurdles (3rd 4x400)

1991   2nd Europa Cup 400m hurdles
1st WAAA 100m hurdles
2nd World Championships 400m hurdles (4th 4x400m)
2nd Grand Prix 400m hurdles
Record holder British and Commonwealth 400m
hurdles

1992   1st AAA 100m hurdles
1st Olympic 400m hurdles (3rd 4x400)

1993   1st Europa Cup 400m hurdles
1st WAAA 100m hurdles

1st World Championships 400m hurdles (3rd 4x400m)
2nd Grand Prix 400m hurdles

Career Record at 400m hurdles

27.6.87	Newham	1	59.9
13.6.88	Padua	1	57.5
24.6.88	Birmingham	2	56.47
23.7.88	Roosendaal	1	56.57
05.8.88	Birmingham	1h2	56.54
06.8.88	Birmingham	1	55.40
28.8.88	Crystal Palace	2	55.00
25.9.88	Seoul Olympics	3h4	55.44
26.9.88	Seoul	4s1	54.48
28.9.88	Seoul	5	54.03
24.6.89	Birmingham	1	56.09
29.6.89	Helsinki	3	55.78
07.7.89	Edinburgh	4	56.13
10.7.89	Nice	3	55.58
14.7.89	Crystal Palace	2	55.43
19.7.89	Pescara	Did not finish (fell)	
05.8.89	Gateshead Europa Cup	2	54.98
16.8.89	Zürich	2	54.64
25.8.89	Brussels	2	55.51
01.9.89	Monte Carlo	3	54.96
08.9.89	Barcelona World Cup	3	55.25
28.1.90	Auckland Commonwealth Games	1h1	56.81

29.1.90	Auckland	1	55.38
27.6.90	Helsinki	1	56.06
29.6.90	Gateshead	2	57.25
04.7.90	East Berlin	3	56.49
20.7.90	Crystal Palace	3	55.72
29.7.90	Lohja	1	55.81
13.8.90	Stockholm	2	55.65
15.8.90	Zürich	4	55.43
29.8.90	Split	2h2	55.89
	European Championships		
30.8.90	Split	3s2	55.35
31.8.90	Split	6	55.45
16.9.90	Sheffield	2	56.93
19.6.91	Crystal Palace	1	55.38
29.6.91	Frankfurt	2	54.61
	Europa Cup		
10.7.91	Lausanne	2	54.76
12.7.91	Crystal Palace	2	55.22
03.8.91	Monte Carlo	1	53.78
07.8.91	Zürich	1	53.62
26.8.91	Tokyo	1h3	54.70
	World Championships		
27.8.91	Tokyo	1s2	54.24
29.8.91	Tokyo	2	53.16
13.9.91	Brussels	1	54.28
15.9.91	Sheffield	1	55.09
20.9.91	Barcelona	4	54.37
04.6.92	St Denis	3	55.80
13.6.92	Crystal Palace	1h1	55.51
14.6.92	Crystal Palace	1	55.33
17.6.92	Verona	1	54.62
19.6.92	Edinburgh	1	55.41

02.7.92	Stockholm	2	54.64
06.7.92	Lille	2	55.20
10.7.92	Crystal Palace	1	54.40
02.8.92	Barcelona	1h4	54.98
	Olympics		
03.8.92	Barcelona	1s1	53.78
05.8.92	Barcelona	1	53.23
14.8.92	Sheffield	1	54.69
19.8.92	Zürich	6	55.04
09.6.93	Rome	1	54.64
26.6.93	Rome	1	53.73
	Europa Cup		
07.7.93	Lausanne	1	53.86
21.7.93	Nice	1	54.29
23.7.93	Crystal Palace	1	53.85
04.8.93	Zürich	1	53.52
16.8.93	Stuttgart	1h1	55.06
	World Championships		
17.8.93	Stuttgart	1s1	53.95
19.8.93	Stuttgart	1	52.74
29.8.93	Sheffield	1	54.25
03.9.93	Brussels	2	54.08
10.9.93	Crystal Palace	2	53.82
18.9.93	Fukuoka	1	54.81

Career Summary

Sally has run a total of 58 races, winning 28. She has never lost to a GB athlete in the 400m hurdles. Setting eight UK records, she has also achieved the fastest twenty-three times in this event.

Acknowledgements

Mum & Dad
I owe it to you not only because I'm here but also because you have made it possible for me to achieve what I have. Even though I've come a long way from that first open meeting, it still means as much to me to know that I have pleased you with a good run.

Joyce & Bigg Daddy
Although this page is too small to list everything you do for us, I want to let you know that it is all much appreciated.

I hope you are enjoying it all as much as we are.

Paul, Cac, Jenny, John & Joanna
Thanks for being so understanding about our busy life. Although we don't see you as much as we would like, it's great to know you're always there.

Martin, Sue & Rosie
Thanks for putting up with all the years of athletics chat – I know where to come to get away from it all.

Bruce

I'll always be grateful to you for starting my athletic career, and helping me achieve my aims.

Matt & Chris

For all the fun and frolics over the years – thanks.

Nanny Camp

You're a great Nan, and I will always be grateful to you for letting me have that special ring.

All my aunts, uncles & cousins

The messages of good luck and congratulations throughout the years have all been very much appreciated – it's great to know that you're all behind me.

Friends

This is my chance to say sorry for not keeping in touch as much as I would like. It's great to see you all from time to time and to be brought back down to earth.

Pannell Kerr Forster

Thanks for all your support and understanding from the very beginning.

Derek Baden

For seeing my potential and believing in me when I really needed it.

David and family

Thank you for the inspiring chats that have helped over the past couple of years.

Everyone at Avon

What a great company – I've made so many new friends. Thank you for helping me move on from Olympic Gold to world record.

Last, but not least, I want to thank M.T.C. for making the whole commercial world easier to understand.

The Publishers would like to thank Panasonic UK for their help in the creation of this book, and Ian Hodge, B.A.F. statistician, for his help with the compilation of the Fact File.

Index